Finding Your Way Home

MELODY LYNN BEATTIE

Finding Your Way Home

---✤---

A SOUL SURVIVAL KIT

Tools for Discovering Your Emotional and Spiritual Power

HarperOne
An Imprint of HarperCollinsPublishers

HarperOne

HarperCollins books may be purchased for educational, business, or sales promotional use. For information please write: Special Markets Department, HarperCollins Publishers, 10 East 53rd Street, New York, NY 10022.

HarperCollins Web Site: http://www.harpercollins.com

HarperCollins®, ▲ ®, and HarperOne™ are trademarks of HarperCollins Publishers.

Library of Congress Cataloging-in-Publication Data

Beattie, Melody.
Finding your way home : a soul survival kit / Melody Beattie.
p. cm.
"Tools for discovering your emotional and spiritual power."
Includes bibliographical references (p.).
ISBN 978–0–06–251118–8
1. Spiritual life.   I. Title.
BL624.B387   1998
291.4'4—dc21   98–21059

10 11 12 13 RRD(H) 31 30 29 28

*This book is for Light Workers
and Light Children.*

CONTENTS

Finding Your Way Home

The change which is upon us
is not a well-kept secret in the Universe.

—BRIAN LUKE SEAWARD IN *THE GOOD REMEMBERING*,
by Lyn Roberts-Herrick

Introduction

Part of my job as a spiritual journalist is to try to listen, be aware, then capture the energy, feelings, and intent buzzing around in the ethers and turn it into a story. If I'm lucky, it turns into a story about healing that a few people can use to help them on their way.

If I get real lucky, it becomes a story that heals me, too.

People are talking a lot lately about the idea of going home. In different ways, shapes, and forms they're expressing the desire to return home. The idea is in the air. Look around. You can see and feel it, too.

They—we—want to go home.

They're not talking about returning to the home of their childhood days. Some don't even know exactly what the desire is they're expressing. It's an idea emanating from the soul, from the deeper part of us, an idea that's found its time.

We want to go home.

It's an itching, a longing, a yearning, a desire bordering on urgency—almost a cosmic movement.

We want to find our purpose, our right place, the right people to live and work with, the right work to do. We want to do more than discover why we're here; we want to be doing and living what we came here to do with the people we came here to do it with. We want to come into alignment with our highest good and destiny.

We want to discover and live our soul's purpose.

We want to bring out and use all the parts of us we've kept denied and tucked away. We don't want to hear anything more about what we can't do. We want to know what we can do, and then we want to do it well. We want to stop exploiting, and start exploring our gifts and talents, bringing them to the world.

And we want to enjoy doing it. We want to have fun. We'd like to make a little money, too. Maybe a lot. It's not that money is the most important thing. We don't want to be bought or sold. Selling our souls is what we want to stop doing. But we want enough. And maybe a little extra at the end of the month. We don't want to worry about money anymore.

We'd like to feel good, do our art, be of service, be with people we love, people of like mind, maybe experience some joy, bliss, and euphoria, too. We want to be part of a team of high-minded soul mates on a similar mission at work; we want a few friends who are truly friends—belong to a tribe of kindred souls; and we want more than a relationship—we want a passionate love relationship with our twin flame soul mate.

Or we want to be happy and comfortable being alone.

We're tired of feeling afraid and confused. We'd like to take some risks, but we'd like to feel safe, too. Protected. We want to live in a way that feels natural and right to us.

We want to be who we are, to be all that our souls came here to be.

We're tired of straitjackets, limitations, and selling our souls for money or security. We want to bust loose—set our souls free, be in the right place at the right time, fulfill our mission, dance with destiny, and watch the universe unfold at our feet.

We want enough drama and excitement to keep life interesting, but we want an abiding sense of peace underlying it all.

Karma and gravity have kept us bound and gagged long enough. We want to return to our spiritual roots. We want to learn to fly.

We want heaven—right here on earth.

That's what I've been hearing. That's what I've been saying, too. *We want to go home.*

It's time to go home—on a cellular, physical, and soul level. Our souls, and the universe, are demanding it.

This is a book about finding your way home—from wherever you are.

It's for homesick people, eager and restless to find that place called home, even—especially—if they're not certain where home is anymore.

It's for people who still believe in angels; in light, color and sound; and in higher beings who come to help. It's for people who believe in music and stories; wishes; destiny; babies; pets; life—after and before death; the holy and the sacred; the sensuous; laughter; themselves; God; this planet; and the rest of the universe, too.

It's for people who believe in a little magic and a lot of love.

It's for people who believe that we, and the world we live in, are multidimensional and that these dimensions are shifting at an intense and determined pace, taking us to a place we haven't yet experienced on this planet—taking us home.

Tucked neatly away under the sink in my bathroom is a small blue polyester bag with a red strap. Inside it is a pair of scissors, gauze, aspirin, an aluminum foil blanket, a make-do shelter, three days of water, and a handful of food supplements. It's an earthquake survival kit, a little something to help me get by in the event of a worst-case scenario (something fairly common recently) in the Los Angeles area, a location I've come to call *home* in the past few years.

Finding Your Way Home is a *soul survival kit*, a little something to ease the discomfort and help us get through these times with our souls intact and our hearts opened.

I suggest reading the book through, cover to cover, to awaken yourself to the ideas contained in it. Then, I recommend using chapters as necessary—prophylactically, routinely, and in the event of spiritual and emotional worst-case scenarios.

At the end of each chapter you will find activities, including guided meditations. You can do these activities when you finish your initial reading of each chapter, to associate and lock in the ideas while they're fresh. Or you can scan them and come back to them later, when you've finished reading all the text. Some activities will appeal to you more than others. Trust yourself about which ones you need and when to do them.

The book is divided into three parts. The first part elaborates on the concept of going home—what that means and how we get there. I wish I could include a map, but I don't have to. You have one in your heart and in the DNA of your soul. It is my hope that reading this book will help release it.

The second part of this book focuses on the doctrines necessary to help us find home. People love rules, step-by-step instructions, concrete guides. *What are the rules for that?* I've been asked, when I suggest opening the heart, freeing our soul, or dancing in harmony with universal love. I'm not certain there are rules, at least not the kind our logical, rational minds would like so we could control things and devise a plan. But we all have doctrines, a set of basic beliefs that become our rules, the laws that we live by. The Doctrines part will help us examine our rules, and change them when change is desirable.

The third part is the fun part. (Actually, all three parts are fun, because going home is fun and feels good—most of the time.) The third part is devoted to remedies. Reading each chapter will help you recall and create the specific mood, climate, or energetic intent of that chapter. Many of you are familiar with the concept of burning a candle to create a particular energy—like tranquillity, creativity, passion, abundance. Some of you may have used aromatherapy, oils, or homeopathic remedies to enhance a particular energy in your life. Each chapter in this part will function like a candle, oil, or homeopath. Read and use the chapters in the Remedy part the way you would burn a candle—to help illuminate what you need at any moment.

For a long time—the better part of my life—I believed (as did many of my peers) that we had to wait passively for the energy we desired to manifest in our lives, whether that desired energy was an insight, a revelation, creativity, tranquillity, love, surrender, emotional healing, joy, bliss, or relief from stress and anxiety (all necessary tools for the homeward bound).

I now believe something different. We can do more than wait. We can do more than cooperate. I believe that we can work with the powers of the universe to cocreate what is desirable and necessary and in our highest good at any point in time. Focused conscious intent—proper exertion of desire and will—isn't optional anymore. It's crucial.

A quickening is at hand—in our lives and on this planet.

In the pages that follow, we'll explore how to work with this new energy while it uproots, urges, nudges, and occasionally forcefully wrests us to that place our souls are calling *home*.

PART 1

The Way Home

Close your eyes,
tap your heels together three times,
and think to yourself,
There's No Place like Home.

—THE WIZARD OF OZ

Toto, I have a feeling we're not in Kansas anymore.

—*THE WIZARD OF OZ*

ONE

It's a Timing Thing

Do you feel confused, uprooted, at a loss—almost depressed, but not quite? Instead of turning with the world naturally and effortlessly as it rotates, is the world spinning around you? Do you feel like it sometimes *turns on you?* Is everything you depended on backing off, fading away? Then, about the time you get your bearings, the world starts turning around *and on* you again?

Are you a little uncertain about what you believe and know to be true, about what life means, how life works, and where your place is in it? Is that fine line between illusion and truth, fiction and nonfiction, fantasy and reality fading—getting fainter and finer each day?

At the risk of using a cliché, *join the crowd.* On second thought, let's regroup. *Join the masses.*

"I don't know what's been going on in the world *and my world* for the past few years," says a forty-three-year-old woman, a successful Midwestern therapist who has worked intensely on her own life and has helped many others. "But most of the time it feels like I'm being pulled through a knothole—backwards."

"For several years now, it feels like I've been plodding through a long, dark tunnel," says a fifty-two-year-old West Coast man, a police officer turned screenplay writer. This man has worked on his spiritual and emotional growth for years. "Sometimes it feels like I'm depressed, but I'm not really depressed. I don't understand what's going on."

"I can't see ahead clearly anymore," says one woman. "Things have been in such a whirl I can barely trust what's going on now. I don't get it. It looks like things are going in one direction, then my course twists and I get slammed into a wall. Remember the old song 'Twist and Shout'? Well, that's my theme song lately. Life takes an ugly twist, and I stand there shouting about it."

The twists and turns life takes lately are enormous, unfathomable, and unpredictable. The only predictable element *is* the twist of unpredictability lurking right around the bend.

A young East Coast woman, a New Yorker, agrees. "You can get whiplash without ever getting into a car. I don't fall asleep at the end of each day," she adds. "I pass out. From stress and obsession."

"I'm going to start making St. John's Wort cookies," chimes in another friend, a man in his thirties. (St. John's Wort is a natural herbal supplement some people claim acts as an antidepressant, the holistic community's response to Prozac.) "No, I'm serious," he says. "I'm going to do it. I've heard that people used to make hashish brownies. There's no reason it can't be done with St. John's Wort."

Someone beat him to the punch. The health food stores are now selling St. John's Wort Tortilla Chips.

The words people use to describe their reactions vary from one locale to another, but the stories I've heard and collected around the globe are similar in content. When I tell people what others are saying, they listen intently, nod their heads in agreement, and respond with one word: *exactly*. Regardless of the language spoken, when I ask what on earth is going on, what sense they make of it, or where it's all leading, they shake their heads, shrug their shoulders, and say, *I don't know.*

In late 1997 I took a research trip through the remnants of the terrorist massacres in Algiers and into the heart of the protest demonstrations in Istanbul, Turkey. While I was sitting in a Swiss airport trying to decide whether to proceed to Bosnia, a television newscast caught my attention. The reporter was standing on the shores of the Pacific along the Malibu coast in California, close to the place I've come to call *home* in the past few years. He was presenting a report on El Niño, the climactic condition named some two hundred years ago for the Christ child. (El Niño usually arrives around Christmas and is a period of unusual global weather patterns resulting from exceptionally warm temperatures in the deep Pacific waters.)

The reporter was interviewing a weather expert, asking what people could expect from this El Niño—more hurricanes, rain-storms, flooding, and consequent mud slides? He tried to nail down an *exact* prediction of what the future held.

The forecaster listened to the interviewer's frantic and insis-tent request, then calmly replied that he thought we'd get about the same weather we usually got, only El Niño would make everything that already existed more intense.

I'm not a weather expert, but that would be an accurate prophecy for the emotional and spiritual climate around our globe.

Things are becoming intense.

In an unpredictable time of twists and turns, when Kodak moments have turned into Prozac moments and the two fa-vorite catch phrases are *exactly* and *I don't know,* another phrase has worked its way into the consciousness.

Going home.

"I'm tired of all the . . . junk," says one woman. "I'm tired of the hustle, not fitting in, not finding my place, and being slightly miserable all the time. I know there's a place on this planet where I can be happy, raise my baby, live by the ocean, and do my art. I just want to find it and move there. I want to go home."

"I've been lying, manipulating, forcing myself into a corporate mold that I don't belong in, and drinking to mask all my motions for a year now," another woman comments. "I've moved from house to house and city to city, but what I've really been doing is running from myself. Enough is enough. It's time to stop running. I miss myself. I want to get comfortable in my own skin. I want my soul back. I want to go home."

"I've allowed myself to be held hostage for years now," confides one man. "I've worked for people I don't like, and I've grown bitter about doing my work, which I used to love. The person that's held me hostage is me. I've been held captive by my own fears and lack of faith—my fears about money and my lack of faith about where I'd go and what I'd do next. It's time to let it all go. It's time to get back in touch with myself and my soul. It's time to go home."

"Something happened to me," says a forty-five-year-old woman, a therapist. "I don't know when it happened or how it happened, but I lost my integrity. And with it, I lost my passion for work and life. I want it back. I want to go home."

"I sold out," another woman states. "I sold out to other people's definitions of what it meant to be successful. I adapted and adapted to people I didn't gel with. I even started to tell myself it didn't matter where I lived or whether or not I had friends in my life. I guess I became convinced I didn't have a place on this planet. I forgot that little things mattered. I got further and further away from myself until I almost forgot who I was, how I felt, and what I wanted. One day, like a rubber band, I couldn't stretch myself any further. I sprang back. I woke up that day, and the lights came on. I saw what I had done, how I had abandoned so many things that were important to me in my quest to climb the corporate ladder. I knew what I had to do. It was time to figure out what I wanted, what was really important to me, and what would feel good and right in my life. Life had become so heavy and hard. It was time to lighten up. It was time to get back to my dreams and to the people and places I was comfortable with. I didn't have to be nearly as miserable as I had become, and then lie to myself about how I really felt or punish myself for feeling that way. I didn't have to be this flexible, adapt this much. I didn't have to be someone I wasn't and try to be that with people I didn't like.

"It was time to go home."

Some people know exactly what they mean by the phrase *going home*, and they're able to articulate that meaning vividly and succinctly. Other people aren't quite so sure what they mean. More than a phrase with one specific meaning, wanting to go home is a feeling—a deep, abiding, universal, and spiritual *feeling*.

One Halloween night years ago, I took my son, Shane, trick-or-treating around our neighborhood. Like many children, he'd been excited all day about wearing his costume and going knocking on doors with other children to show people how he was dressed and to collect his candy in return. After about an hour and a half of walking up and down stairs, knocking on doors, and having groups of other children race by making ghoulish sounds, Shane was finished.

"I don't want to knock on any more doors. I don't want any more candy. I don't want to wear this costume anymore," he said, ripping the mask off his face. "I just want to go home."

That's the feeling I hear being expressed.

There's an old story that's been circulating around Hollywood for years, about the agent who gets buzzed by his assistant on the phone, then told that a man named Lucifer wants to talk to him on line three.

"I don't know any guy named Lucifer," the agent says.

"Well, he says he knows you," the assistant says, "and he says he needs to talk to you now."

The agent mumbles a bit, then picks up the phone and says hello.

"Have I got a deal for you," Lucifer says. "In exchange for your eternal soul, I'll give you all the money, power, and sex you want."

"Just a minute," the agent says. "Let me make sure I got this right. You're telling me all I have to do is give you my soul, and in return, you'll give me all the money, power and sex I want. I'm not stupid. What's the catch?"

The catch, of course, is how important our souls are.

People are tired of selling themselves. They want their *souls* back. They want to go home.

How important, or real, is the soul? We stand at the edge of a technological and scientific breakthrough that will allow humankind to create and duplicate life in all its forms and shapes by cloning. Daisy, the cloned sheep, even became pregnant. The implications of this breakthrough are mind-boggling concerning life on this planet, loss, grief, and death. Cloning, it is claimed, will make it possible to recreate a specific person from a lock of his or her hair and an egg from the maternal ovary.

Yet, standing at this threshold we balk in an indecision bordering on terror. What if the person we recreate is duplicated perfect in every detail *but lacks a soul?* The implications of this are even more mind-boggling.

That's how important a soul is.

That's how important each of our souls is.

How important is the soul, spirit, or essence of a corporation, an organization, or an institution? Go to work for an organization or place yourself in the care of an institution that has no spirit or whose essence has been deadened, numbed, or contaminated—or is in conflict with the values of your own soul. That question, too, will be quickly answered.

People need more than a body, and corporations and institutions need more than a financial bottom line.

It's the spirit of a thing that counts overall. And this is a book about connecting with the power of spirit—our soul—and allowing that connection to lead us to the best place for each of us in our daily lives.

This is a book about finding your way home. That can mean finding the best city—or country—to live in, the best people to live and associate with, the best work to do. But it's about more than that. It's a book about making a solid, tangible connection with your soul and, through that connection, finding your own way home each day.

Can we make conscious contact with our souls? Can the process be taught, learned, reduced, and distilled into a how-to book or a weekend workshop? I believe we can get messages and guidance from a book—and from any other source in the universe that we're led to. As to whether or not we can connect with our souls and get on the homeward-bound path, I'm not certain how much choice we have anymore.

This connection to our souls can't be bought, manipulated, or forced. And it will not be indefinitely ignored.

The mysterious veil separating our conscious mind from our subconscious or Super Conscious—and ultimately the living consciousness of our universe—is being thinned.

It's a timing thing.

Do you feel like you're being pulled through a knothole backward? Maybe you are, and it's squeezing out all your fears. Feel like you're plodding through a long, dark tunnel? Could it be you're pushing through the darkness so you can get to the other side and see and appreciate the light? Is life twirling you around in circles, then pushing you blindfolded onto a path? Maybe it's to shake you out of your rut, challenge your values, stir up your emotions, and show you how much you already know about finding your way home.

Something is in the air, in the winds, in the weather, in the rain. And it's more than the effects of El Niño. These aren't times that *try men's souls.* These are the times that *set them free.*

ACTIVITIES

Create a soul survival kit. Just as many of us have earthquake survival kits, or emergency kits of various kinds, we can create a soul survival kit. We can choose a backpack, velvet bag, or box to contain items that have spiritual, or soul, meaning to us. Or we can create the *kit* in our imaginations and leave the items scattered throughout our home, knowing that these are the elements that go in our imaginary kit—the one we're creating to help our souls survive. Throughout this book, I'll encourage you to make lists of various activities that nurture your soul. I'll also encourage you to search out items that speak to your soul, and have meaning to you. These items—and other essentials such as your journal and a dream workbook—will all become tools in your kit. The important idea here is not to create a specific bag to use for a kit, although that can be sweet and helpful. The idea is to begin thinking in terms of items and activities that speak to, nourish, and nurture our souls.

Help bridge the gap between your conscious mind and your soul with a guided meditation. This one is simple but powerful. Read it until you're familiar with it, then get in a comfortable position, either sitting or lying down. Close your eyes and visualize it in your mind until you can see the picture clearly and can see yourself in the picture.

> *Picture yourself standing at the entrance to a bridge, a walkway across a chasm. You can make the bridge as high or as low or as wide or narrow as you want. But to get to the other side, you need to step onto the bridge and walk across. The side you're standing on is a little dark. It's familiar, but it's not where you want to be anymore. Even if you have some fear, envision yourself feeling excited and curious to get to the other side. You may not be able to see what's on the other side clearly yet, but it looks greener, lighter, happier over there. Feel your desire and determination to cross the bridge.*
>
> *Picture yourself walking, safely taking each step, or running (if you want to run) across the bridge. Stay with yourself each step of the way. Hold the railing if you like, or run freely down the middle of the bridge. But take each step until you get to the other side. When you get to the other side, keep walking until you are completely off the bridge and your feet are planted on solid ground. Give yourself a moment to look back at where*

you've come from. Smile and wave at anyone, or anything, you've left behind. Bless them. Release them. Don't worry about who you've left behind; when they're ready to cross, their bridge will appear. Turn around, smile, and take a moment to enjoy the beauty you see and feel on this new side.

Know you're safe. You have successfully crossed the bridge. Your feet are planted on solid ground. Feel yourself surrounded by people who love you. You may not be able to see their faces or recognize who they are yet, but you can feel their love. Feel yourself surrounded by trees, mountains, sunshine, and birds. You may not know exactly what you're going to find on this new side, but you feel secure. Know and trust that it will be good.

Whenever life gets too intense, reach into your soul survival kit and retrieve this picture. See yourself safely across the bridge, on the other side, liking what you feel and trusting what you can't yet clearly see.

probably already alerted your regular salesgirl that you are coming, and the hostess will ring to tell her you've arrived. If not, you will be assigned a salesgirl for your visit. The salesgirls are known as Dasluzettes and are the daughters of São Paolo's best families. They are *très soigné*—tall and thin, with smooth butternut skin and long glistening hair—and they move in the city's rarefied social circles, attending smart dinner parties and extravagant galas nightly. "The salesgirls live the life that the customers live," Tranchesi explained. "So they understand."

If you're a regular customer, chances are your Dasluzette has already pulled several pieces that you will probably love and put them aside in a private salon for you to try on. New clothes arrive often, which is why Daslu's best customers tend to come to the store four times a week. "Women in Brazil are completely crazy about fashion," Mendes told me during my visit. "Clients buy American *Vogue*, tear out the pages, give them to the salesgirl and say, 'When that arrives, I want it.' When the Fendi Baguette first came out, we sold them all in presale before we received them."

If you are a new customer, like I was, your Dasluzette will give you a tour, collecting items that interest you as you move from room to room. Like the old Daslu, the store layout is like a house with interconnecting salons. The decor is in soft off-white tones with thick champagne-hued carpeting—it's as if you've plunged into a vat of *crème anglaise*—and white orchids everywhere. On the ground floor are the designer boutiques, including all the regular suspects: Vuitton, Dior, Gucci, Valentino, Jimmy Choo, Sergio Rossi, Chloé, Pucci, Valentino, Manolo Blahnik. "Every young Brazilian woman knows Manolo Blahnik," Tranchesi said with a laugh. "And Valentino sells well because the husbands love their wives in Valentino dresses." For most of the brands, Daslu owns the franchise and chooses the clothes. But the brands usually handle the decor themselves, to maintain continuity; Peter Marino designed the Chanel and Dolce & Gabbana boutiques. Vuitton, Burberry, Armani, and Ferragamo lease their space from Daslu. The Vuitton store, at four thousand square feet, is the largest in Latin America.

On the second floor you'll find fine jewelry, perfume, lingerie, swimwear, vintage wear, a few more luxury brands, a champagne bar, the Leopolldina restaurant, and Daslu private label for women, known as Daslu Collection. No men are allowed in the Daslu women's department, and there are security guards posted at the entrances to make sure. There are no dressing rooms on the women's floor. Instead, customers strip down to their lacy underwear and try on the clothes right there on the sales floor. "My mother only received friends, so there was no problem changing in front of one another," Tranchesi explained. "I did the same: friends receiving friends, so no need for changing rooms. It's natural for Brazilians. You aren't ashamed if men aren't around."

The Daslu collection has become a pillar of the store. It accounts for 60 percent of sales there and is now carried by several international retailers including Bergdorf Goodman, Saks-Jandel in Washington, Tracey Ross in L.A., and Harrods and Browns in London. Tranchesi still designs the collection and has it made in Brazil, mostly in locally produced materials. The clothes are casual chic: swishy jersey dresses, sexy stretch jeans, towering strappy sandals decorated with big faux jewels, filmy gowns flecked with crystals. As you settle into one of the cozy corners with comfy sofas to try them on, the maids, known as the "uniform girls" because of their black dresses with white aprons and stockings, will serve you refreshments. "When Daslu was in my mother's house, the maids, who wore the same uniform, helped and served," Tranchesi explained. "They started by giving coffee or water. Then they started to put the clothes back." Now there is an army of three hundred.

The ambiance at Daslu is clubby and delightfully upbeat. Customers come from Rio and Salvador, Argentina and Peru. Everyone knows everyone—there are plenty of air kisses. They shop for a few hours, meet up for high tea in the Leopolldina restaurant or for a drink in the champagne bar, catch up on gossip, then shop some more. Six times a year, Daslu hosts a festive fashion show/party for ten thousand of its best customers. "The women dance, shop, and have a great time," Mendes says. On Tuesday evening, Daslu stays open until ten, and chic Paulistas meet there for dinner and shopping. The wealthy and famous like Daslu, she explained, "because you have a lot of privacy, you have everything you need, and everyone is treated like a VIP." Celebrities particularly like the safety of the Daslu compound. "Nothing happens to them here," Mendes said. "No one notices or bothers them. [Formula One champion] Michael Schumacher came here last year and nobody said anything. [Brazilian soccer star] Ronaldo is one of the most important clients we have at Daslu and nothing happens. No autographs. No photos. Nothing." A few years ago, Tranchesi had a study done of shopping habits at Daslu. "Normally, in a Brazilian shopping mall, 20 percent buy," she told me. "At Daslu, 75 percent of people who walk inside buy something."

On the third floor is the men's department. There's a Johnnie Walker whiskey bar, a bookstore with a fireplace and sofas, and even a La Perla lingerie boutique, "so they can buy for their wives and girlfriends," Mendes says. There's a men's Daslu ready-to-wear line; departments dedicated to electronics, athletic wear, and gym equipment; a travel agency; a luxury real estate agency; Mitsubishi, Volvo, and Maserati dealerships; a Ferretti yacht broker; a Daslu helicopter dealer (one hangs on display in the atrium); a tobacconist; a music department; a Japanese restaurant called Kosushi that is considered the best in São Paolo; and a wine department with a selection of vintages to rival the best caves in Paris.

On the fourth floor, you find the children's clothing and toy department, with a playroom and a kid's-height bar with bowls of gumdrops and plates of chocolate chip cookies, a bank, a pharmacy where you can fill your prescriptions, a hairdresser where each client has a private room, and a spa: "Brazilian women are crazy about the body and skin care—it's unbelievable," Mendes said. "They have facial massages regularly." Daslu of course has the best facialist in town. "It takes four or five months to get an appointment." She adds. In addition, there is Casa Daslu, with table-, glass-, and silverware as well as refrigerators, barbecues, and a Viking showroom; a stationer to do your engraved notepaper and invitations; a chocolate shop run by Tranchesi's sister, where all the chocolates are made by hand; and a bakery called Pati Piva that does extravagant tiered wedding cakes. On the ground level, there is a consecrated wedding chapel, and on the fifth floor is a series of immense terrace-like reception rooms and a ballroom that can seat thirteen hundred, all with a view of the city. "I think Daslu is the only place in Brazil where you can do everything for your wedding, including holding the ceremony and the reception, booking the honeymoon, and buying the house," Mendes said.

When it is time to pay, you are ushered into a lounge-like room where you sit on one of the comfortable Louis XVI chairs, have a coffee brought to you by a uniform girl, and chat with your salesgirl while everything is run up. On the counter sits a pile of the latest Daslu CDs, a compilation by the Daslu deejay of hip Brazilian and Latin music, which you can buy for a few reales. On the wall is a flat-screen TV broadcasting Daslu TV. Throughout the store, Daslu radio is playing. You pay the bill and are escorted out by your Dasluzette, empty-handed. Everything has been sent down to your car, or up to the helipad.

There are seven hundred Daslu employees, including the uniform girls; a thousand others employed by brand shop-in-shops, travel agencies, restaurants, and so on; and nine hundred third-party service providers such as valets, janitors, and security guards. Next door, Daslu has an employee day care center called the Villa Daslu Educational Center with a nursery where female staff can come and nurse their babies three times a day, and a school for children up to age fourteen. Some two hundred attend. The children receive instruction in English, art, sewing, piano, guitar, and ballet—often by clients. When I visited the school, I met two tall, elegant clients who had just finished teaching a group of eight-year-old girls in the ballet studio. There is also a pediatrician, a dentist, and a psychologist. After a hot lunch in the school cafeteria, children seven and older go to the local public school. Younger children stay and play. They have snack time on picnic benches in the garden. "The uniform girls were unhappy with the schools and the quality of life for their children, so we opened the school," explained Mendes as we walked down the hallway and visited classes. "This is even better than my children's school."

But what really sets Daslu apart from other luxury retailer's is Tranchesi's personal involvement with the business. Chances are, you'll run into her while you are shopping, and she'll ask how the kids are, help you pick out a few things, or assist in fittings. "In America, in Europe, retailers know what they've sold by looking at the numbers in the computer," she told me. "I know what we sell here because I'm on the shop floor. I don't sit in an office. I run the business from here"—and she tapped her belly. "In luxury brand stores, when you pay, they forget about you. They completely forget about you," Mendes told me. "Eliana doesn't just know the name of the client, she *knows* the client. Daslu is her house, and the customers are her guests."

Shortly after the opening at the new location in July 2005, Daslu was raided by federal police agents and Tranchesi was arrested for alleged tax evasion. The government alleged that import-export firms falsified invoices listing prices of imported goods far below market value to allow Daslu to pay less in duty. "It was crazy—280 police came to the office," said Mendes. "You never see that in a *favela*, even when there is a big drug trafficking bust. But Daslu, yes. It was to show off in the press, to draw attention from Lula and his problems," she said, referring to President Luis Inacio Lula da Silva, the country's socialist president, who has been embroiled in a series of corruption scandals. Tranchesi was released shortly after. In December 2006, Daslu was ordered to pay $110 million in back taxes. The store planned to appeal.

On the second day I went to Daslu—it took three entire days to see the place—I had lunch with one of its good customers, a chic woman named Cristiane Saddi, the marketing director for the local Mercedes dealership that her husband owns. She also volunteers at a local Syrian-Lebanese hospital that her grandmother and her great-aunt founded. Saddi is one of those remarkable women who give Brazil its reputation as the land of stunningly sensual women: thin, tan, and taut, with long black hair as slick as oil and eyes to match, she was dressed in a tight white Dolce & Gabbana blazer over a lacy white camisole, skinny white Diesel jeans, big diamond stud earrings, and towering heels. We met in Leopolldina, Daslu's elegant restaurant and one of São Paolo's top power spots, packed daily with celebrities, businessmen, and socialites. The chef is Italian, and the cuisine is a Best of Europe tour: filet mignon with red wine sauce, wild mushroom risotto, lobster-stuffed ravioli, prosciutto and melon, and seviche.

We talked of her Daslu experience. "My mother used to go to the original one and would take me," Saddi said as she tucked into an ample lunch of beef filet and pasta. "I started shopping there myself when I was fifteen. Now I'm forty-three. It grows and grows and never loses that family feel. You're not received as a client but as a family friend. When I got married, we lived just down the street. I would call and say, 'I need a gift for this or that,' and they would pull something. Salesgirls are your friends. They are in the same social swirls. When you go to Daslu, it's not to buy a new pair of shoes. It's to see your friends. You can't find this service anywhere else in the world."

And we talked about life as a São Paolo socialite: "You can be everything all together—work, mother, hostess—because you have staff," she said. "In return, you help with the schools, houses, everything. My driver has been with me twenty-one years, since I married, and I have watched his children grow up. When he was sick I put in him in the hospital and got him the best doctors, the best treatments. You help them, because they help you. All the families here do that. It's an exchange."

What I really wanted to know, though, was this: what, for Cristiane Saddi, is luxury today?

"Daslu is a luxury because you can do what you want," she explained, pouring dark chocolate sauce over two slices of cake. "They have the best brands and the best choice in the world, from bras to evening gowns to housewares. Everything you need for everything. How many fashion stores also sell cars? You just think about a product—you can buy it at Daslu."

After two days at Daslu, I understood what she meant. Daslu may have been dreamy, but it wasn't a dream.

As she dug into her cake, I began to think about the state of the luxury business, how it seemed over the last two decades to have lost its soul. I wondered where it would go: what would it do once the Japanese and Americans had grown weary of luxury brands and emerging markets were saturated? When gimmicks like art galleries and gala concerts would no longer draw crowds in the stores? When there were no more corners to cut and there was no more growth to be had? Was there enough integrity or value left in these brands to allow them to continue to call themselves "luxury"? Or, more important, to maintain their legitimacy, I asked Saddi, would they be able to keep the wealthy like her and her peers as customers?

"Yes," she said. "The Louis Vuitton here carries only its most expensive items," she said. "Daslu clients don't need the logo entry-level handbag or to wear labels or logos. We buy from luxury brands, but not ordinary products. Special items. There's always something special. You can see what is mass and what is special. Luxury is not how much you can buy. Luxury is the knowledge of how to do it right, how to take the time to understand and choose well. Luxury is buying the *right thing*."

And with that, Saddi wiped the chocolate off her lips, reapplied her lipstick, got up, and kissed me good-bye.

"Must get back to work," she said, and she clicked off in her stilettos.

ACKNOWLEDGMENTS

Deluxe exists thanks in large part to two extraordinary women: Nina Hyde, the legendary fashion editor of the *Washington Post,* who gave me my first job as a fashion reporter in the late 1980s, and taught me that fashion was as serious and respectable a beat as covering the White House; and Amy Spindler, style editor of the *New York Times Magazine,* who assigned me a series of major investigative pieces about the fashion industry in the late 1990s, and said to me, "You should turn this into a book." She was right. Sadly, like Nina Hyde a decade earlier, Amy Spindler succumbed to cancer far too young and before she could see it happen.

Peter Riva helped shape the idea for *Deluxe* and gave me the kick I needed to sit down and write the proposal. My agent, Tina Bennett at Janklow & Nesbit, had the patience to keep rereading it for what seemed like forever until it sparkled, then sent it to Ann Godoff and Emily Loose at Penguin Press in New York and Stefan McGrath at Penguin Press in London, who—on my fortieth birthday, no less—courageously took me on and guided me into authorhood. Penguin Press editors Jane Fleming and Helen Conford tag-teamed me, asking all the right questions and adding needed structure, both to me and the manuscript. Happily, their interpretation of "a couple of more months" was as elastic as mine.

Deluxe would not contain half the information it has without *Newsweek*. My editors Fareed Zakaria, Nisid Hajari, and Susan Greenberg and my Paris bureau chief Christopher Dickey allowed me to wander the planet on behalf of the magazine in search of the real story behind the luxury industry, and published early versions of these reportages in *Newsweek*'s international edition. Sue Greenberg further gave up weekends and part of her New Year's vacation to gently shape the manuscript into a seamless read, as she has done with my *Newsweek* copy for more than a decade. Longtime *Newsweek* Paris bureau photo editors Ginny Power and Jacqueline Duhau helped to choose and find just the right pictures to accompany my words and popped up my spirits when they started to wane.

A slew of young, hungry reporters helped me with research, including Marie Valla, Jenny Barchfield, Remi Hoki, J. J. Martin, Erin Zaleski, Florence Villeminot, Nicole Martinelli, Laura Czigler, and Lauren Greenwald. These dynamic young women spent hours chasing down obscure numbers, setting up interviews in far-flung places, and, when needed, translating foreign languages. Fact-checker supreme Austin Kelley pored through mountains of documents, deciphered my scribble, and followed up with sources to make sure I got it right. And several luxury brand PR folks—including Amee Boyle at Giorgio Armani, Olivier Labesse at DGM Conseil, Marie-Louise de Clermont-Tonnere and Claire Chassard at Chanel, Annelise Catineau and Olivier Monteil at Hermès and the unflappable Nathalie Tollu at Louis Vuitton—answered my seemingly endless barrage of follow-up questions with speed and aplomb. I could have never pulled this book together without them.

I am deeply grateful to the hundreds of people I interviewed for *Deluxe* on the record, including Wanda McDaniel, Kenneth Fang,

Tom Ford, Laudomia Pucci, Kris Buckner, Handel Lee, Menehould de Bazelaire, Leslie Caron, and Olivia de Havilland, and those who spoke to me off the record and told me the secrets of the luxury industry. Mônica Mendes was right to insist that I travel to São Paolo to see Daslu firsthand, and was extraordinarily welcoming when I did, and Jennifer Woo and Bonnie Brooks of Lane Crawford, Wilfred Koo of Givenchy, and David Tang helped me negotiate Hong Kong and Guangzhou, making what seemed impossible achievable. Several friends, including Laurie Sprague, Cathy Nolan, Kevin Mulvey, and Mike Medavoy, read *Deluxe* in rough form or debated its premise with me, and their input shaped its outcome. I must also thank photographers Don Ashby, Marcio Madeira, and Patrick Demarchelier and artist Tom Sachs for generously providing beautiful images for *Deluxe,* Andre Balazs, Philip Pavel and everyone at the Chateau Marmont for putting up with me as I tried to channel the hotel's writing ghosts, and the indefatigable June Newton, who kindly invited me into her home and took the most honest portrait of me ever.

More than once while reporting and writing *Deluxe* I thanked the heavens above for allowing me to start my journalism career in the Style section of the *Washington Post*—the writer's section of the writer's newspaper—during the reign of the *formidable* Ben Bradlee. Editors Mary Hadar, Deborah Heard, Rose Jacobius, and Gene Weingarten and music critic Joseph McLellan took me as a green and eager college student, gave me terrific assignments, and pushed me to dig deeper and write better. It was journalism boot camp and finishing school all in one, and I use all that they taught me every day of my career.

Most important, I could have never written *Deluxe* without the encouragement of my family and the profound support and love of my husband, Hervé, and our incredibly patient daughter, Lucie—my light—who gamely accompanied me on many of my reporting adventures and spent half of her six-year life waiting for me to finish this project.

Now, honey, now we can go play in the park.

NOTES

INTRODUCTION

Page

3   **The luxury goods industry:** Claire Kent, luxury goods analyst, Morgan Stanley London, e-mail, April 18, 2005.

3   **Thirty-five major brands:** Claire A. Kent et al., "Making the Sale," Morgan Stanley Dean Witter, March 11, 1999, p. 10.

4   **In Asia:** David B. Yoffie and Mary Kwak, "Gucci Group N.V., (A)" Harvard Business School, case 9–701–037, September 19, 2000; revised May 10, 2001, p. 4.

6   **The Chinese enriched:** Palmer White, *The Master Touch of Lesage: Embroidery for French Fashions* (Paris: Editions du Chêne, 1987), p. 16.

7   **As Diana Vreeland:** Diana Vreeland, *D.V.* (New York: Da Capo Press, 1997), p. 47.

7   **"I'm no philosopher":** Stanley Karnow, *Paris in the Fifties* (New York: Random House, 1997), p. 263.

10   **In 2005:** "Best & Most 2005," Generation DataBank, www.generation.se.

11   **In their best year:** Rana Foroohar, with Mac Margolis in Rio de Janeiro, "Maximum Luxury," *Newsweek Atlantic Edition,* July 25, 2005, p. 44.

11   **The Swiss bank:** Rana Foroohar, "Going Places," *Newsweek International,* May 15–May 22, 2006, p. 54.

11   **The private security:** Ibid., p. 58.

12   **By 2011:** Foroohar, "Maximum Luxury," p. 44.

12   **When Arnault:** Deborah Ball, "Decisiveness and Charisma Put Yves Carcelle in the Hot Seat at LVMH's Principal Division," *Wall Street Journal Europe,* October 1, 2001, p. 31.

13   **"What I like":** "Arnault, in His Own Words," *Women's Wear Daily,* December 6, 1999, p. 11.

CHAPTER ONE: AN INDUSTRY IS BORN

17   **"Luxury is a necessity":** Anna Johnson, *Handbags: The Power of the Purse* (New York: Workman, 2002), p. 21.

18   **Its flagship:** Eric Wilson, "Optimism's the Point, Not Excess Baggage," *New York Times,* October 13, 2005, p. G1.

18   **"Luxury is crossing":** Joshua Levine, "Liberté, Fraternité—but to Hell with Egalité!" *Forbes,* June 2, 1997, p. 80.

20   **"High profitability":** Suzy Wetlaufer, "The Perfect Paradox of Star Brands," *Harvard Business Review,* October 2001, p. 123.

22   **Louis XIV dressed:** Stanley Karnow, *Paris in the Fifties* (New York: Random House, 1997), p. 268.

22   **Louis XVI's wife:** Judith Thurman, "Dressed for Excess: Marie-Antoinette, Out of the Closet," *New Yorker,* September 25, 2006, p. 138.

22   **She was "an object":** Palmer White, *The Master Touch of Lesage: Embroidery for French Fashion* (Paris: Editions du Chêne, 1987), pp. 20–21.

22   **"French fashions":** Karnow, *Paris in the Fifties,* pp. 268–69.

23   **At the age of thirteen:** Paul-Gérard Pasols *Louis Vuitton: The Birth of Modern Luxury,* (New York: Abrams, 2005), p. 13.

23   **The 292-mile trek:** Ibid., p. 21.

23   **"Here you find":** Ibid., p. 24.

23   **Vuitton became:** Ibid., p. 30.

23   **In 1854:** Ibid., p. 354.

23   **Throughout the mid-1800s:** White, *Master Touch of Lesage*, p. 24.

24   **"Women will stoop":** Karnow, *Paris in the Fifties*, p. 270.

24   **Worth's dresses:** White, *Master Touch of Lesage*, pp. 24–25.

24   **His prices:** Karnow, *Paris in the Fifties*, p. 271.

24   **Louis Vuitton's business:** Pasols, *Louis Vuitton*, p. 88.

26   **To keep up with:** Ibid., p. 76.

26   **"In those days":** Maria Riva, *Marlene Dietrich: By Her Daughter* (New York: Knopf, 1993), p. 111.

26   **In the 1920s, France:** White, *Master Touch of Lesage*, p. 56.

27   **In five years:** Ibid., p. 51.

27   **In the 1930s:** Ibid., p. 62.

27   **"The huge skirt":** Diana Vreeland, *D.V.* (New York: Knopf, 1984), p. 98.

27   **But couturier Lucien:** Marie-France Pochna, *Christian Dior: The Man Who Made the World Look New* (New York: Arcade, 1996), p. 78.

27   **"You can force us":** Ibid., p. 77.

28   **The Vuittons were:** Kim Willsher, "Louis Vuitton's Links with Vichy Regime Exposed," *Guardian,* June 3, 2004, p.15.

28   **"The styles [during]":** Karnow, *Paris in the Fifties*, pp. 266–67.

29   **I remember Ivana:** Nina Hyde, "Lacroix's Curtain-Raising Couture; Kicking Off the Fall Shows with Soft Chiffon & Crepe," *Washington Post*, July 24, 1988, p. G1.

30   **The swanlike models:** Karnow, *Paris in the Fifties*, pp. 258–59.

30   **"After all the horrors":** Ibid., p. 264.

30   **The Parisian clients:** Ibid., p. 263.

32   **Couture houses:** Ibid., p. 260.

33   **By 1951:** White, *Master Touch of Lesage*, p. 80.

33   **Soon licensing:** Richard Morais, *Pierre Cardin: The Man Who Became a Label* (London: Bantam, 1991), p. 91.

33   **"I was staying":** Vreeland, *D.V.*, pp. 106–7.

34   **"Bloomingdale's":** Ibid., p. 134.

34   **By 1977:** Nadège Forestier and Nazanine Ravaï, *The Taste of Luxury: Bernard Arnault and the Moët-Hennessy Louis Vuitton Story* (London: Bloomsbury, 1992), p. 54.

35   **Finally, in 1977:** Hugh Sebag-Montefiore, *Kings on the Catwalk: The Louis Vuitton and Moët-Hennessy Affair* (London: Chapmans, 1992), p. 82.

35   **He decided:** Ibid., p. 16.

36   **Recamier expanded:** Pasols, *Louis Vuitton*, p. 280.

36   **In 1984:** In 1984, Vuitton sales were 1.25 billion French francs and profits were 197 million French francs. Chris Hollis (Investor Relations, LVMH), e-mail with the author, February 5, 2007.

36   **In 1986:** Sebag-Montefiore, *Kings on the Catwalk*, p. 115.

CHAPTER TWO: GROUP MENTALITY

41   **The result:** Suzy Wetlaufer, "The Perfect Paradox of Star Brands," *Harvard Business Review,* October 2001, p. 122.

42   **The France:** Jennifer Steinhauer, "The King of Posh," *New York Times*, August 17, 1997, Sec. 3, p. 1.

42   **"You have to":** Joshua Levine, "Liberté, Fraternité—but to Hell with Egalité!" *Forbes,* June 2, 1997, p. 80.

42   **Upon graduating:** Nadège Forestier and Nazanine Ravaï, *The Taste of Luxury: Bernard Arnault and the Moët-Hennessy Louis Vuitton Story* (London: Bloomsbury, 1992), p. 10.

43   **Arnault fled:** Ibid., pp. 13–14.

44   **"I can be":** Ibid., p. 11.

44   **Its only hope:** Hugh Sebag-Montefiore, *Kings on the Catwalk: The Louis Vuitton and Moët-Hennessy Affair* (London: Chapmans, 1992), pp. 23–24.

44   **He convinced Lazard:** Levine, "Liberté, Fraternité," p. 80.

45   **It was perhaps:** Sebag-Montefiore, *Kings on the Catwalk,* p. 41.

45   **He shocked:** David D. Kirkpatrick, "The Luxury Wars," *New York Megazine,* April 26, 1999, p. 24.

45   **Unlike Dior's:** Sebag-Montefiore, *Kings on the Catwalk,* pp. 30–31.

45   **When he took:** Forestier and Ravaï, *Taste of Luxury,* p. 17.

46   **"I don't want":** Sebag-Montefiore, *Kings on the Catwalk,* p. 37.

47   **In 1988:** Nina Hyde, "The Battle of Lacroix," *Washington Post,* April 7, 1988, p. C1.

47   **Feeling beaten:** Sebag-Montefiore, *Kings of the Catwalk,* pp. 50–58.

48   **In the spring:** Ibid., p. 137.

48   **At one point:** Ibid., p. 220.

48   **The French daily:** Forestier and Ravaï, *Taste of Luxury,* p. 93.

48   **Finally, in April:** Sebag-Montefiore, *Kings on the Catwalk,* p. 232.

49   **His motivation:** Forestier and Ravaï, *Taste of Luxury,* p. 106.

49   **He expanded:** Wetlaufer, "The Perfect Paradox," p. 121.

49   **Carcelle was:** Deborah Ball, "Decisiveness and Charisma Put Yves Carcelle in the Hot Seat at LVMH's Principle Division," *Wall Street Journal Europe,* October 1, 2001, p. 31.

50   **"You think of Vuitton":** Zoe Heller, "Jacob's Ladder," *New Yorker,* September 22, 1997, p. 109.

52   **"If you control":** Levine, "Liberté, Fraternité," p. 80.

52   **By 2004:** "LVMH: Full of Potential, Will It Be Realized?" Merrill Lynch, November 2002.

52   **Dior's sixty-three-year-old:** Sebag-Montefiore, *Kings on the Catwalk,* p. 192.

53   **"[Audrey] Hepburn":** Kirkpatrick, "The Luxury Wars," p. 24.

53   **In 1996:** Levine, "Liberté, Fraternité," p. 80.

54   **"For a European":** Steinhauer, "King of Posh," p. 1.

54   **"[Arnault] is":** Ibid., p. 1.

56   **He travels:** John Marcom Jr., "The Quiet Afrikaner behind Cartier," *Forbes,* April 2, 1990, p. 114.

56   **"We concentrate":** William Hall, "Companies & Finance: When Time Is a Business's Ultimate Luxury," *Financial Times,* June 9, 2000, p. 34.

56   **"It's not just about":** James Fallon, "Rupert's Way: While Competitors Spend for Acquisitions Like There's No Tomorrow, Richemont CEO Johann Rupert Plans for a Rainy Day," *Women's Wear Daily,* May 30, 2000, p. 8S.

57   **"Product integrity":** Ibid.

57   **"We are not":** Hall, "Companies & Finance," p. 34.

57   **"In five to ten":** Fallon, "Rupert's Way," p. 8S.

57   **Cartier accounts for:** Miles Socha, "Milking Fashion's Cash Cows," *WWD The Magazine,* November 3, 2003, p. 88.

58   **By the late 1980s:** Kirkpatrick, "Luxury Wars," p. 24.

58   **"It was pretty much":** David Yoffie and Mary Kwak, "Gucci Group N.V. (A)," Harvard Business School case (9–701–037), May 10, 2001, p. 2.

59   **Gucci sales:** Ibid., p. 9.

60   **De Sole declared:** Kirkpatrick, "Luxury Wars," p. 24.

60   **Arnault said:** Ibid.

60   **Pinault laughed:** Sarah Raper, "LVMH's Arnault: The Tower and the Glory," *Women's Wear Daily,* December 6, 1999, p. 8.

61   **When PPR took:** Yoffie and Kwak, "Gucci Group N.V. (A)," p. 14.

65   **Her father, Gino:** Myriam de Cesco, "Galeotta fu una borsa," *Lo Specchio,* January 8, 2000, pp. 76–80.

65   **"We passed":** Ibid.
68   **"It can be":** Michael Specter, "The Designer," *New Yorker,* March 15, 2004, p. 112.
68   **Once Bertelli:** Cathy Horyn, "Prada Central," *Vanity Fair,* August 1997, p. 96.
69   **By the end of 2001:** Specter, "The Designer," p. 114.

CHAPTER THREE: GOING GLOBAL

76   **In February 1976:** Kyojiro Hata, *Louis Vuitton Japan: The Building of Luxury* (New York: Assouline, 2004), p. 7.
76   **"The serenity":** Ibid., p. 11.
77   **Hata came:** Ibid., p. 23.
78   **"During the first ten years":** Ibid., p. 75.
79   **But the economic boom:** Claire Kent, Sarah Macdonald, Mandy Deex, and Michinori Shimizu, "Back from Japan," Morgan Stanley Equity Research, Europe, November 14, 2001, pp. 3, 7.
80   **They were the only:** Ilene R. Prusher, "Japanese Retailers Turn to 'Shetailers,'" *Christian Science Monitor,* August 29, 2001, p. 1.
80   It was a wise: Deborah Ball, "Decisiveness and Charisma Put Yves Carcelle in the Hot Seat at LVMH's Principal Division," *Wall Street Journal Europe,* October 1, 2001, p. 31.
82   **In 2006:** www.moodiereport.com/pdf/tmr_may_06_6.pdf.
82   **In 1960:** Stephanie Strom, "LVMH to Buy Duty-Free Empire for $2.47 Billion," *New York Times,* October 30, 1996, p. D1.
82   **Between 1977 and 1995:** Judith Miller, "He Gave Away $600 Million, and No One Knew," *New York Times,* January 23, 1997, p. A1.
83   **"This was not":** Jon Nordheimer, "Slaughtering the Cash Cow: Millions of Dollars Couldn't Keep DFS Group Together," *New York Times,* March 12, 1997, p. D1.
83   **Feeney, the more:** Miller, "He Gave Away $600 Million," p. A1.
83   **Miller, by contrast:** Jerry Adler, "He Gave at the Office," *Newsweek,* February 3, 1997, p. 34.
83   **In 1994:** David D. Kirkpatrick, "The Luxury Wars," *New York Magazine,* April 26, 1999, p. 24.
83   **Feeney and Parker:** Vicki M. Young, "Miller Threatens Suit after LVMH Pulls Out of Talks for DFS Stake," *Women's Wear Daily,* March 20, 1997, p. 1.
85   **In 2003:** "Japanese International Travelers: Trends and Shopping Behavior," 2003 JTM/TFWA Japanese Traveler Study, Executive Summary, p. 1.
88   **"Andy was":** Joshua Levine, *The Rise and Fall of the House of Barneys* (New York: Morrow, 1999), p. 118.
88   **For those who:** Ibid., p. 199.
91   **"Rule No. 1":** Kate Betts, "The Retail Therapist," *Time,* May 30, 2005, p. 53.
91   **Sales at the Osaka:** Ibid.
91   **After Marino renovated:** Miles Socha, "King Louis: Louis Vuitton's New Clothing Store," *Women's Wear Daily,* October 10, 2005, p. 1.
92   **Hata has long:** Hata, *Louis Vuitton Japan,* pp. 40–43.
93   **"It's luxury":** Elizabeth Heilman Brooke, "Tokyo Club: A New Way to Shop," *International Herald Tribune,* February 27, 2004, p. 14.
95   **The total cost:** "Chanel Opens Flagship Shop in Tokyo's Ritzy Ginza," Agence France Presse, December 4, 2004.

CHAPTER FOUR: STARS GET IN YOUR EYES

101   **Gucci nearly:** David B. Yoffie and Mary Kwak, "Gucci Group N.V. (A)," Harvard Business School, case 9-701-037, September 19, 2000; revised May 10, 2001, p. 10.
101   **LVMH spent:** Federico Antoni, "LVMH in 2004: The Challenges of Strategic Integration," Stanford Graduate School of Business, case SM–123, March, 17, 2004, p. 12.

102 **"We are the largest":** David D. Kirkpatrick, "The Luxury Wars," *New York Magazine,* April 26, 1999, p. 24.

102 **At Gucci:** Yoffie and Kwak, "Gucci Group N.V. (A)," p. 10.

103 **Silent-screen siren:** Patty Fox, *Star Style: Hollywood Legends as Fashion Icons* (Santa Monica, Calif.: Angel City Press, 1995), pp. 76–77 and pp. 83–90.

104 **When Crawford:** Ibid., p. 24.

104 **Grace Kelly's:** Ibid., p. 96.

104 **Hollywood stars:** Ibid., p. 92.

104 **sold their signatures:** Marian Hall, with Marjorie Carne and Sylvia Sheppard, *California Fashion: From the Old West to New Hollywood* (New York: Abrams, 2002), p. 92.

104 **He originally settled:** Salvatore Ferragamo, *Shoemaker of Dreams: The Autobiography of Salvatore Ferragamo* (Florence: Giunti Gruppo Editoriale, 1985), pp. 37–48.

105 **In the early 1920s:** Ibid., pp. 51–54.

105 **"Valentino would drop":** Ibid., pp. 89–92.

106 **But in 1955:** Marie-France Pochna, *Christian Dior: The Man Who Made the World Look New* (New York: Arcade, 1996), pp. 161–162.

107 **For most of the twentieth century:** Scott Huver and Mia Kaczinski Dunn, *Inside Rodeo Drive: The Store, the Stars, the Story* (Santa Monica, Calif.: Angel City Press, 2001), p. 12–18.

109 **The Gucci store:** Sara Gay Forden, *The House of Gucci; A Sensational Story of Murder, Madness, Glamour, and Greed* (New York: HarperCollins, 2001), p. 39.

110 **By the late 1970s:** Anthony Cook, "Wheeling and Dealing on Status Street," *New West,* February 27, 1978, p. 20.

110 **Beverly Hills:** Ibid., p. 19.

110 **Hayman was once:** Karen Stabiner, "Spring Fashion: King of the Hills," *Los Angeles Times Magazine,* February 15, 1998, p. 18.

112 **The neighborhood boys:** Judy Bachrach, "Armani in Full", *Vanity Fair,* October 2000, p. 193.

114 **Fred Pressman:** Joshua Levine, *The Rise and Fall of the House of Barneys* (New York: Morrow, 1999), p. 90.

114 **In 1979:** Michael Kaplan, "Blame It on Armani," *Movieline,* September 19, 1999, p. 74.

115 **When *Time*:** Levine, *House of Barneys,* p. 92.

118 ***Vogue*'s Anna Wintour:** Author interview, Paris, July, 2001.

118 **Jennifer Meyer:** Jareen Stabiner, "Dressing Well Is the Best Revenge," *Los Angeles Times Magazine,* December 11, 1988, p. 42.

122 **"Those girls":** Gaby Wood, "She's Got the Look," *Observer,* July 16, 2006, p. 12.

124 **Zoe has even:** Booth Moore, "In Her Image: Rachel Zoe's Clients (Lindsay, Nicole, Jessica) Often Look Like . . . Her," *Los Angeles Times,* July 16, 2005, p. E1.

126 **According to a study:** *Lifestyle Monitor,* January, 2005.

127 **Sir Elton:** Shawn Hubler and Gina Piccalo, "The Heirarchy," *Los Angeles Times,* March 1, 2005, p. E5.

129 **One prominent stylist:** Libby Callaway, "Red Carpet Catfighting: The Seamy Side of the Stars' Style Wars," *New York Post,* February 29, 2004, p. 48.

129 **One stylist reportedly:** "Fat Chance," *People Hollywood Daily,* February 26, 2005, p. 14.

132 **Chopard's:** Booth Moore, "Red Carpet Revenue," *Los Angeles Times,* February 22, 2005, p. E12.

CHAPTER FIVE: THE SWEET SMELL OF SUCCESS

135 **"A woman enveloped":** Janet Wallach, *Chanel: Her Style and Her Life* London: Mitchell Beazley, 1999), p. 162.

139 **"[Dior's perfume]":** Federico Antoni, "LVMH in 2004: The Challenges of Strategic Integration," Stanford Graduate School of Business, case SM–123, March, 17, 2004, p. 6.

140 **Prehistoric man:** Diane Ackerman, *A Natural History of the Senses* (New York: Random House, 1990), pp. 56–59.

140 **In Crete:** Ibid., pp. 60–61.

141 **French king Louis XIV:** Ibid., p. 62.

144 **"The industry has":** Caroline Brothers, "The Precise Smell of Success," *International Herald Tribune,* October 21–22, 2006, p. 12.

144 **In 2003:** Miles Socha, "Milking Fashion's Cash Cows," *WWD the Magazine,* November 3, 2003, p. 88.

145 **She was born in:** Wallach, *Chanel,* pp. 5–18.

145 **She made her way:** Ibid., pp. 19–31.

146 **First she did a test:** Alex Madsen, *Chanel: A Woman of Her Own* (New York: Henry Holt, 1990), p. 135.

147 **Théophile Bader:** Ibid., p. 136.

147 **Throughout the 1920s:** Stanley Karnow, *Paris in the Fifties* (New York: Random House, 1997), p. 273.

149 **Her first collection:** Wallach, *Chanel,* p. 150.

149 **Even Christian Dior:** Ibid., p. 154.

153 **Together, they do:** Chandler Burr, "The Scent of the Nile," *New Yorker,* March 14, 2005, p. 78.

153 **In late 2006:** Brid Costello and Matthew W. Evans, "Givaudan-Quest: Creating a New Number One," *Women's Wear Daily,* November 27, 2006, p. 3.

154 **Take Dior's brief:** Burr, "Scent of the Nile," p. 78.

162 **"All I see":** "Fashion Scoops: In the Flesh," *Women's Wear Daily,* July 11, 2001, p. 5.

164 **They can be:** Burr, "Scent of the Nile," p. 87.

164 **When Alain Lorenzo:** Joshua Levine, "Liberté, Fraternité—but to Hell with Egalité!" *Forbes,* June 2, 1997, p. 80.

CHAPTER SIX: IT'S IN THE BAG

169 **Handbags have:** Andrea Lee, "Bag Lady," *New Yorker,* September 25, 2006, p. 80.

169 **"It's like you've":** Anna Johnson, *Handbags: The Power of the Purse* (New York: Workman, 2002), p. 54.

169 **I read about:** Reggie Nadelson, "Out of the Box," *Departures,* May–June, 2002, p. 146.

169 **In September 2005:** Ben Widdicombe, "Gatecrasher," *New York Daily News,* September 10, 2005, p. 20.

170 **At the Venice Biennale:** Farid Chenoune, *Carried Away: All About Bags* (Paris: Le Passage Paris—New York Editions, 2004), p. 72.

171 **Jackie Onassis:** Nadelson, "Out of the Box," p. 143.

171 **Maryvonne Pinault:** Ibid., p.176.

171 **Carrying into a jury:** Robin Givhan, "Martha's Moneyed Bag Carries Too Much Baggage," *Washington Post,* January 22, 2004, p. C1.

173 **Among the more:** Nadelson, "Out of the Box," p. 146.

173 **In 2003:** Pascale Renaux, "L'Ange Guardian," *Numéro,* October 2003, p. 302.

174 **"We are frightened":** Nadelson, "Out of the Box," p. 150.

174 **Whereas Gucci Group's:** Lisa Lockwood, "Polet's Prescription for Changing Gucci," *Women's Wear Daily,* November 16, 2005, p. 45.

174 **In 1995:** Christopher Dickey, "C'est Chic, C'est French," *Newsweek International,* March 17, 1997, p. 38.

181 **This persecution:** Nadelson, "Out of the Box," p. 177.

184 **As he likes:** Dickey, "C'est Chic, C'est French," p. 38.

184 **Sales were so slow:** Bridget Foley, "Full Galop," *W,* March 1998, p. 230.

184 **He found the rue:** Helmut Newton, *Autobiography* (New York: Doubleday, 2003), pp. 241–42.

186 **The modern handbag:** Chenoune, *Carried Away,* passim.

187 **"Listen, Diana":** Diana Vreeland, *D.V.* (New York: Knopf, 1984), p. 89.

187 **It had no monogram:** Johnson, *Handbags,* p. 7.

188 **"We've got into the":** Chenoune, *Carried Away,* p. 32.

189   **In 1986:** Palmer White, *The Master Touch of Lesage: Embroidery for French Fashion* (Paris: Editions du Chêne, 1987), p. 134.

191   **As Holly Brubach:** Holly Brubach, "In Fashion: Forward Motion," *New Yorker,* June 25, 1990, p. 77.

193   **It became:** Andrea Lee, "Bag Lady," *New Yorker,* September 25, 2006, p. 80.

194   **Market sources:** Miles Socha, with contributions by Jennifer Weil, "LVMH Profits Pass $1 Billion," *Women's Wear Daily,* March 10, 2005, p. 9.

196   **Between 1994 and 1998:** David B. Yoffie and Mary Kwak, "Gucci Group N.V. (A)," Harvard Business School, case 9–701–037, September 19, 2000; revised May 10, 2001, p. 11.

199   **That year, Frankfort:** Barbara Woller, "First-Class Coach," *Journal News,* May 23, 2005, p. 1D.

199   **From 2001 to 2006:** Claire A. Kent, Mandy Deex, Rachel Whittaker, Angela Moh, and Andy Xie, "Luxury Goods in China: A Long-Term Investment," Morgan Stanley, February 27, 2004, p. 13.

202   **A brown leather tag:** Alessandra Galloni, Cecilie Rohwedder, and Teri Agins, "Foreign Luxuries: Breaking a Taboo, High Fashion Starts Making Goods Overseas," *Wall Street Journal,* September 27, 2005, p. A1.

202   **In May 2005:** Adam Jones, "Prada Ponders Outsourcing to China," *Financial Times,* May 20, 2005, p. 10.

CHAPTER SEVEN: THE NEEDLE AND THE DAMAGE DONE

209   **It has been used:** Nina Hyde, "Silk, the Queen of Textiles," *National Geographic,* January 1984, p. 48.

213   **Back in the 1920s:** Pietra Pietrogrande, *Antico Setificio Fiorentino* (Florence, Italy: Le Lettere, 1999), p. 71.

213   **Back in the factory's:** Ibid., p. 95.

214   **On some farms:** Hyde, "Silk, the Queen of Textiles," pp. 14–19.

214   **The Chinese began:** Ibid., pp. 27–30.

215   **One recounts:** Ibid., p. 36.

215   **Another tells:** Pietrogrande, *Antico Setifico Fiorentino,* p. 21.

215   **One of the early centers:** Ibid., pp. 33–43.

221   **In 2004:** Alessandra Galloni, Cecilie Rohwedder, and Teri Agins, "Foreign Luxuries: Breaking a Taboo, High Fashion Starts Making Goods Overseas," *Wall Street Journal,* September 27, 2005, p. A1.

227   **One-fourth of Hong Kong's:** Ted C. Fishman, *China Inc.* (New York: Scribner, 2005), p. 88.

227   **By the mid-1990s:** Ibid., p. 89.

228   **In September 2006:** "In Brief: Actor Appeals to Burberry," *Women's Wear Daily,* November 27, 2006, p. 2.

228   **In November:** David Cracknell and Jonathan Leake, "Charles Joins the Burberry Revolt," *Times* (London), November 26, 2006, p. 4.

229   **Peter Hain:** Samantha Conti, "Burberry to Close Factory," *Women's Wear Daily,* January 11, 2007, p. 15.

229   **Today, there are:** "Swatches: Canton Connection," *Women's Wear Daily,* January 3, 2006, p. 8.

229   **China's textiles:** John Zarcostas, "China's Textile Exports Soar 23.8 Percent," *Women's Wear Daily,* January 10, 2006, p. 8.

230   **In late 2005:** George Wehrfritz, "A River in Reverse," *Newsweek International,* January 30, 2006, p. 53.

231   **The constant pressure:** John Zarocostas, "Global Labor Study Cites Human Rights Violations," *Women's Wear Daily,* October 19, 2005, p. 19.

232   **"Chinese factories":** Jane Perlez, "Vietnam Arrives as an Economic Player in Asia," *International Herald Tribune,* June 20, 2006, p. 2.

232   **"China is no longer":** Luisa Zargani, "China Trains Eye on Italian Firms," *Women's Wear Daily*, February 22, 2006, p. 13.

CHAPTER EIGHT: GOING MASS

239   **America Online:** Annie Groer, "The New Gilded Age," *Washington Post*, August 1, 1999, p. F1.

239   **According to a University:** Juliet B. Schor, *The Overspent American: Why We Want What We Don't Need* (New York: HarperPerennial, 1999), p. 14.

239   **According to a Roper:** Ibid., p. 16.

239   **Since 1970:** Michael J. Silverstein and Neil Fiske, with John Butman, *Trading Up: The New American Luxury* (New York: Portfolio, 2003), pp. 25–26.

239   **By 2005:** Sharon Edelson, "Chasing Big Spenders: Stores Step Up Services for Key Luxe Customers," *Women's Wear Daily*, August 1, 2006, p. 1.

239   **Between 1979 and 1995:** Schor, *Overspent American*, p. 12.

239   **According to a 1997 study:** Ibid., 159.

239   **Between 1990 and 1996:** Ibid., p. 72.

239   **Yet it wasn't enough:** Ibid., p. 6.

240   **In 2004:** "Accessible Luxury—What It Is and Why It's Working," Ledbury Research, November 8, 2004.

241   **"When we look":** David D. Kirkpatrick, "The Luxury Wars," *New York Magazine*, April 26, 1999, p. 24.

244   **And MGM Mirage:** Sharon Edelson, "Taubman Plans for Big Names at Vegas Center," *Women's Wear Daily*, September 21, 2005, p. 5.

247   **"It was jolting":** Karen Heller, "On Deep Discount, Prada Has Never Looked Worse," *Philadelphia Inquirer*, January 6, 2006, p. M3.

247   **"The 1980s":** Booth Moore, "Outlet for That Energy," *Los Angeles Times*, September 1, 2005, p. 28.

249   **"I once got home":** Laura Landro, "Style—Hunting & Gathering: Catwalk Chic on the Cheap," *Wall Street Journal*, September 17, 2005, p. 11.

250   **But, says Linda Humphers:** Moore, "On Deep Discount," p. 28.

250   **But the average:** Ibid.

251   **"The winning formula":** Ibid.

254   **"The luxury industry":** Vanessa Friedman, "An Online Business Model Dressed to Kill," *Financial Times*, May 30, 2006, p. 10.

254   **It ran a huge overhead:** Karen Lowry Miller, "Hitting the Wall at Boo," *Newsweek Atlantic Edition*, July 17, 2000, p. 42.

259   **Analysts believe:** Cathy Horyn, "Point, Click and Strut," *New York Times*, December 15, 2005, p. 1.

259   **Furthermore, Forrester:** Luca S. Paderni, with Jaap Favier and Manuela Neurauter, "Louis Vuitton Takes Online Luxury Shopping Mainstream," Forrester Research, November 8, 2005.

260   **The primary culprits:** Lisa Bertagnoli, "To Catch a Thief: Independent Retailers Forgo High Tech Gizmos and Gadgets in Favor of Old-Fashioned Security Measures," *Women's Wear Daily*, October 13, 2004, p. 58S.

260   **Luxury's most famous:** Adam Tschorn, "Hollywood's Walk of Shame," *Women's Wear Daily*, February 24, 2004, p. 34S.

260   **"It's not normal":** Guy Trebay, "Shoplifting on a Grand Scale: Luxury Wear Stolen to Order," *New York Times*, August 8, 2000, p. B1

260   **In Minnesota:** Schor, *Overspent American*, p. 40.

260   **Andrew McColl:** Trebay, "Shoplifting," p. B1.

260   **At times, robberies:** Rosemary Feitelberg, "Two Nabbed in Versace Hold-Up; Boston Boutique Site of Armed Robbery," *Women's Wear Daily*, May 12, 1997, p. 23.

261   **The pros:** Trebay, "Shoplifting," p. B1.

261   **"They obviously":** Greg Lindsay, "Sticky Fingers," *Women's Wear Daily,* January 27, 2004, p. 23.

261   **Chavs are:** Rob Walker, "The Good, the Plaid and the Ugly," *New York Times Magazine,* January 2, 2005, p. 20.

263   **As Kim Hastreiter:** Kim Hastreiter and David Hershkovits, *Twenty Years of Style: The World According to Paper* (New York: Harper Design International, 2004), p. 34.

263   **Logos—particularly:** Teri Agins, *The End of Fashion: How Marketing Changed the Clothing Business Forever* (New York: Quill, 2000), p. 111.

263   **Gianni Versace:** Ibid., p. 139.

263   **"What can we do?":** Gideon Rachman, "Bubbles and Bling," *Economist,* Summer 2006, p. 20.

264   **"I view":** George Rush and Joanna Molloy, "Daily Dish," *New York Daily News,* June 15, 2006, p. 26.

266   **In 2001:** Scott, Huver and Mia Kuczinski Dunn, *Inside Rodeo Drive: The Store, the Stars, the Story* (Santa Monica, Calif.: Angel City Press, 2001), p. 34.

CHAPTER NINE: FAUX AMIS

273   **In 1948:** Stanley Karnow, *Paris in the Fifties* (New York: Random House, 1997), pp. 260–61.

274   **In 1982:** International Anti-Counterfeiting Coalition, white paper, January 2005, p. 3.

274   **In 2004:** Ted C. Fishman, "Manufaketure," *New York Times Magazine,* January 9, 2005, p. 40.

275   **In 2002:** IACC white paper, p. 20.

276   **Prada CEO:** Robin Progrebin, "Reality Check," *Connoisseur,* n.d., p. 140.

281   **As Jasper Becker:** Jasper Becker, *The Chinese* (New York: Free Press, 2000), pp. 74–75.

282   **A month later:** Evan Clark, "U.S. Report Calls for Action on Intellectual Property Laws," *Women's Wear Daily,* May 2, 2005, p. 16.

285   **That same month:** "U.S. Charges 17 with Trafficking in Counterfeit Goods, Money Laundering, Attempted Bribery of a Public Official," United States Attorney Southern District of New York, press release, June 4, 2004.

285   **The street value:** Progrebin, "Reality Check," p. 140.

285   **The same is true:** Peter S. Goodman, "In China, a Growing Taste for Chic; But Fakes Also Vex Developing Market," *Washington Post,* July 12, 2004, p. A1.

292   **Many of the street-level:** Marcus Mabry and Alan Zarembo, "Africa's Capitalist Jihad," *Newsweek Atlantic Edition,* July 7, 1997, p. 42.

293   **During a two-day:** Julia Preston, "U.S. Charges 51 with Chinatown Smuggling," *New York Times,* November 13, 2004, p. B2.

CHAPTER TEN: WHAT NOW?

299   **In 2006:** Emily Flynn Vencat, "Shaping the New Looks," *Newsweek International,* May 15–22, 2006, p. 82.

299   **In 2004:** Paul Klebnikov, "Russia's Richest People: The Golden Hundred," Forbes.com, July 22, 2004.

300   **The Chinese didn't:** Claire A. Kent, Mandy Deex, Rachel Whittaker, Angela Moh, and Andy Xie, "Luxury Goods in China: A Long-Term Investment," Morgan Stanley, February 27, 2004, p. 4.

300   **"It's cheaper":** Lisa Movius, "Shanghai's Bund 18 Luring Luxury Brands," *Women's Wear Daily,* January 11, 2005, p. 18.

303   **By 2004:** Kent, Deex, Whittaker, Moh, and Xie, "Luxury Goods in China," p. 6.

303   **"In other provinces":** Sarah Mowar, "Dressed to Shanghai," *Vogue,* October 2004, p. 336.

303   **"We are still":** Lisa Movius, "China's Luxury Rush: Expanding Vuitton Shows Market's Growth," *Women's Wear Daily,* December 29, 2005, p. 12.

304   **By the end of 2006:** Amanda Kaiser, "Tilling the Luxury Landscape," *Women's Wear Daily,* March 21, 2006, p. 2B.

304   **Calvin Klein:** Lisa Movius, "Valentino Unveils Women's for Mainland China," *Women's Wear Daily,* September 26, 2006, p. 17.

304   **Since its arrival:** Zhu Ling, "Louis Vuitton to Open Three New Stores in China," www.chinadaily.com.cn/bizchina/2006–05/15/content_589908.htm, May 15, 2006.

306   **Mainland China:** Luisa Zargani, "Luxury and the Lands of Opportunity," *Women's Wear Daily,* November 29, 2004, p. 4.

306   **"Three years ago":** Lisa Movius, "Bulgari Continues Expanding in China," *Women's Wear Daily,* September 29, 2006, p. 22.

307   **"Mainlanders go":** Tom Miller, "Shopping Is the Lure for Mainlanders," *South China Morning Post,* November 7, 2005, p. 16.

307   **Mainlanders are enrolling:** Howard W. French, "In China, the Upper-Class Quest Starts Low—at Age 5," *International Herald Tribune,* September 22, 2006, p. 1.

307   **"I have customers":** "Seeking Russian Gold: Despite Turmoil, Brands Rush to Booming Market," *Women's Wear Daily,* September 30, 2004, p. 1.

308   **At many of Armani's:** Miles Socha, "Couture's New Hope: Russia, Asia and the Mideast," *Women's Wear Daily,* January 23, 2006, p. 5.

308   **Outside of Moscow:** Natasha Singer, "Russia's Luxury Mania: Stores Grab Real Estate to Build New Empires," *Women's Wear Daily,* October 4, 2004, p. 1.

308   **After the 1998:** Robert Galbraith, "Courting the New Russian and Indian Luxury Consumers," *International Herald Tribune,* September 30, 2005, p. 14.

309   **For the Dior opening:** Miles Socha and Brid Costella, "Christian Dior's New Flagship on Red Square," *Women's Wear Daily,* October 24, 2006, p. 3.

309   **Nearby, Mercury Group:** Singer, "Russia's Luxury Mania," p. 1.

309   **"Before we designed":** Ibid.

310   **Christian Dior reported:** "Seeking Russian Gold," p. 1.

311   **In 2005:** Galbraith, "Courting the New Russian and Indian Luxury Consumers," p. 14.

311   **"People have the money":** Rosemary Feitelberg, "On to India, China," *Women's Wear Daily,* December 5, 2006, p. 17.

311   **There are more:** Ibid.

312   **A study by Bain:** Ibid.

312   **The most coveted:** Cecily Hall, "Far East Fashion-Forward," *Women's Wear Daily,* June 1, 2006, p. 12.

312   **"In just the last year":** Betsy Lowther, "The Treasures of India: As Luxe Brands Rush In, Prime Space Runs Out," *Women's Wear Daily,* November 7, 2006, p. 1.

312   **Analysts at McKinsey:** Vencat, "Shaping the New Looks," p. 82.

312   **"The chance of":** Amy S. Choi, "Eyeing India's Riches: As Barriers Come Down, Luxury Brands Go Slow," *Women's Wear Daily,* March 13, 2006, p. 1.

313   **State governments:** Ritu Upadhyay, "Bombay Dispatch: Expanding Malls," *Women's Wear Daily,* March 13, 2006, p. 11.

313   **The finance ministry:** Choi, "Eyeing India's Riches," p. 1.

314   **"It's a PR machine":** "Talk about Branding," *Time,* June 2005, Bonus Section, p. A4.

315   **"Our hotels":** J. J. Martin, "Travel with Style," *Harper's Bazaar,* Fall 2006, p. 89.

316   **Fashion darling:** Miles Socha, "Philo Said Working with Gap," *Women's Wear Daily,* November 27, 2006, p. 2.

318   **Burberry began:** Claire Kent, Mandy Deex, Elke Finkenauer, Rachel Whittaker, "Luxury & Apparel Retail," Morgan Stanley Equity Research Europe, March 7, 2005, p. 17.

318   **Mizrahi calls:** Ibid., p. 10.

CHAPTER ELEVEN: NEW LUXURY

321   **In early 2006:** Amanda Kaiser, "Jil Sander Loss Hits $46.3 Million in 2005," *Women's Wear Daily,* May 30, 2006, p. 3.

322   **"All these big":** Sarah Raper, "LVMH's Arnault: The Tower and the Glory," *Women's Wear Daily,* December 6, 1999, p. 8.

322   **Burberry CEO:** "Continental Compensation," *Women's Wear Daily,* July 17, 2003, p. 14.

322   **according to *Forbes*:** www.forbes.com/lists/2006/12/Rank_1.html.

322 **"A mobile phone":** Luisa Zargani, with contributions by Alessandra Ilari, "Prada Calling Via Venture with LG," *Women's Wear Daily,* December 13, 2006, p. 11.

323 **"She says":** Holly Brubach, "In Fashion: Forward Motion," *New Yorker,* June 25, 1990, p. 79.

334 **The wealthiest:** Sharon Edelson, "Chasing Big Spenders: Stores Step Up Services for Key Luxe Customers," *Women's Wear Daily,* August 1, 2006, p. 1.

334 **Danielle Morolo:** Ibid.

334 **"My best customer":** Ibid.

335 **Saks Fifth Avenue:** Ibid.

BIBLIOGRAPHY

Ackerman, Diane. *A Natural History of the Senses*. New York: Random House, 1990.

Agins, Teri. *The End of Fashion: How Marketing Changed the Clothing Business Forever*. New York: Quill, 2000.

Arnault, Bernard. *La Passion Créative: Entretiens avec Yves Messarovitch*. Paris: Plon, 2000.

Becker, Jasper. *The Chinese*. New York: Free Press, 2000.

Bindloss, Joseph; Sarina Singh; Deanna Swaney; and Robert Strauss. *Mauritius, Réunion & Seychelles*. Victoria, Australia: Lonely Planet, 2001.

Bloch, Phillip. *Elements of Style: From the Portfolio of Hollywood's Premier Stylist*. New York: Warner, 1998.

Bonvicini, Stéphanie. *Louis Vuitton: une saga française*. Paris: Fayard, 2004.

Brubach, Holly. *A Dedicated Follower of Fashion*. London: Phaidon Press, 1999.

Burr, Chandler. *The Emperor of Scent: A Story of Perfume, Obsession and the Last Mystery of the Senses*. New York: Random House, 2002.

Celant, Germano, and Harold Koda. *Giorgio Armani*. New York: Solomon R. Guggenheim Foundation, 2000.

Chenoune, Farid. *Carried Away: All About Bags*. Paris: Le Passage Paris—New York Editions, 2004.

Ferragamo, Salvatore. *Shoemaker of Dreams: the Autobiography of Salvatore Ferragamo*. Florence, Italy: Giunti Gruppo Editoriale, 1985.

Fishman, Ted C. *China, Inc.* New York: Scribner, 2005.

Forden, Sara Gay. *The House of Gucci: A Sensational Story of Murder, Madness, Glamour, and Greed*. New York: HarperCollins, 2001.

Forestier, Nadège, and Nazanine Ravaï. *The Taste of Luxury: Bernard Arnault and the Moët-Hennessy Louis Vuitton Story*. London: Bloomsbury, 1992.

Fox, Patty. *Star Style: Hollywood Legends as Fashion Icons*. Santa Monica, Calif.: Angel City Press, 1995.

Galbraith, John Kenneth. *The Affluent Society,* New York: Houghton Mifflin, 1998.

Hall, Marian, with Marjorie Carne and Sylvia Sheppard. *California Fashion: From the Old West to New Hollywood*. New York: Abrams, 2002.

Hastreiter, Kim, and David Hershkovits. *20 Years of Style: The World According to* Paper. New York: Harper Design International, 2004.

Hata, Kyojiro. *Louis Vuitton Japan: The Building of Luxury*. New York: Assouline, 2004.

Huver, Scott, and Mia Kuczinski Dunn, *Inside Rodeo Drive: The Store, the Stars, the Story.* Santa Monica, Calif.: Angel City Press, 2001.

Johnson, Anna. *Handbags: The Power of the Purse*. New York: Workman, 2002.

Karnow, Stanley. *Paris in the Fifties*. New York: Random House, 1997.

Kennedy, Shirley. *Pucci: A Renaissance in Fashion*, New York: Abbeville Press, 1991.

Krannich, Ronald L. *The Treasures and Pleasures of China: Best of the Best*. Manassas Park, Va.: Impact Publications, 1999.

Levine, Joshua. *The Rise and Fall of the House of Barneys*. New York: Morrow, 1999.

Madsen, Alex. *Chanel: A Woman of Her Own*. New York: Henry Holt, 1990.

Mally, Ruth Lor. *China Guide*, Cold Spring Harbor, N.Y.: Open Road Publishing, 2002.

Morais, Richard. *Pierre Cardin: The Man Who Became a Label*. London: Bantam, 1991.

Newton, Helmut. *Helmut Newton, Autobiography*. New York: Doubleday, 2003.

Pasols, Paul-Gérard. *Louis Vuitton: The Birth of Modern Luxury*. New York: Abrams, 2005

Pietrogrande, Pietra. *Antico Setificio Fiorentino*. Florence, Italy: Le Lettere, 1999.

Pochna, Marie-France. *Christian Dior: The Man Who Made the World Look New*. New York: Arcade, 1996.

Rawsthorn, Alice. *Yves Saint Laurent*. London: HarperCollins, 1996.

Riva, Maria. *Marlene Dietrich: By Her Daughter*. New York: Knopf, 1993.

Schor, Juliet B. *The Overspent American: Why We Want What We Don't Need*. New York: HarperPerennial, 1999.

Sebag-Montefiore, Hugh. *Kings on the Catwalk: The Louis Vuitton and Moët-Hennessy Affair*. London: Chapmans, 1992.

Silverstein, Michael J., and Neil Fiske, with John Butman. *Trading Up: The New American Luxury*. New York: Portfolio, 2003.

Smith, Sally Bedell. *Reflected Glory: The Life of Pamela Churchill Harriman*. New York: Simon & Schuster, 1996.

Twitchell, James B. *Living It Up: Our Love Affair with Luxury*. New York: Columbia University Press, 2002.

Veblen, Thorstein. *The Theory of the Leisure Class*. New York: Penguin, 1994.

Vreeland, Diana. *D.V.* New York: Da Capo Press, 1997.

Wallach, Janet. *Chanel: Her Style and Her Life*. London: Mitchell Beazley, 1999.

Watson, Albert. *Prada a Milano*, Milan: Grafica di Italia Lupo.

White, Palmer. *The Master Touch of Lesage: Embroidery for French Fashion*. Paris: Editions du Chêne, 1987.

INDEX

PHOTO CREDITS

A TALE OF TWO
GARDENS

THE NEW DIRECTIONS *Bibelots*

OCTAVIO PAZ

A TALE OF
TWO GARDENS

Poems from India 1952-1995

EDITED AND TRANSLATED BY ELIOT WEINBERGER

With additional translations by Elizabeth Bishop,
Paul Blackburn, Lysander Kemp, Muriel Rukeyser, and
Charles Tomlinson

A NEW DIRECTIONS

Publisher's note: Except for "Kavya: 10 Epigrams from the Sanskrit,"
which is newly translated into Spanish by Octavio Paz, all the
poems from East Slope and Toward the Beginning in this volume
appear in The Collected Poems of Octavio Paz: 1957–1987, first
published by New Directions clothbound in 1987. An excerpt from
"Mutra" appeared in Early Poems, 1935–1955, first published by
New Directions in 1973, and is here presented in its entirety. Paz's
long note to "Mutra" and Eliot Weinberger's introduction were
written especially for this book.

Manufactured in the United States of America
First published as a New Directions Bibelot in 1997
New Directions Books are printed on acid-free paper.
Published simultaneously in Canada by Penguin Books Canada
Limited

Library of Congress Cataloging-in-Publication Data
Paz, Octavio, 1914–
    A tale of two gardens : poems from India / Octavio Paz ; edited
by Eliot Weinberger.
       p.   cm.
    ISBN 0-8112-1349-8 (alk. paper)
    1. Paz, Octavio, 1914–   —Translations into English.   2. India—
Poetry.   I. Weinberger, Eliot.   II. Title.
PQ7397.P285A29   1997
861—dc21   96–38111
                                                          CIP

New Directions Books are published for James Laughlin
by New Directions Publishing Corporation,
80 Eighth Avenue, New York 10011

Contents

KEY TO TRANSLATORS

[MR] = Muriel Rukeyser
[CT] = Charles Tomlinson
[PB] = Paul Blackburn
[LK] = Lysander Kemp
[EB] = Elizabeth Bishop
All others by Eliot Weinberger

Introduction

For forty years, India has been the twin of Mexico in Octavio Paz's life and work: the *other* to his self-described otherness as a Mexican. He first went to India in 1951 as a minor functionary in Mexico's first diplomatic legation to the new Republic. He stayed for six months, and the poem that opens this book, "Mutra" (here accompanied by a recent long note), was his first response to what he saw, thought, was overwhelmed by.

In 1962 he returned as the Mexican ambassador, responsible not only for India, but also for Afghanistan, Pakistan, Nepal, and, as it was called at the time, Ceylon. He was to remain for six years, traveling widely, studying Indian philosophy and art, and—"After being born, the most important thing that has happened to me"—meeting and marrying Marie-José Tramini. In 1968, he resigned his post to protest his government's massacre of peaceful student demonstrators in Mexico City shortly before the Olympic Games were held there.

Out of these years came an extraordinary series of books: *Alternating Current,* with its essays on Buddhist logic, Hinduism, and caste; *Conjunctions and Disjunctions,* his meditation on Eastern and Western concepts of the body and non-body; and *The Monkey Grammarian,* his erotic "unraveling novel" of a pilgrimage to Galta in Rajasthan. He also organized the first exhibition of Tan-

tric art in the West. Above all, in India he wrote the poems of *East Slope* (*Ladera este*), which are universally considered among the finest in the more than sixty years of his continuing writing life.

East Slope is in three sections. The first, "East Slope," opens with the lines "Stillness/ in the middle of the night"—the poet is alone on a balcony overlooking Old Delhi—and then it immediately fills, overflows, with Indian things: monuments, landscapes, a jungle of specific flora and fauna, painters, musicians, gardens, gods, palaces, tombs, philosophy, temples, history, bits of Indian English, and strange characters. In section two, "Toward the Beginning," this exuberant world stops ("The present is motionless") and is encompassed by the poet and his lover/wife in a series of intense erotic lyrics: the passion that, in Hindu Tantrism, leads to liberation. It ends, in "A Tale of Two Gardens," with the couple in the middle of the ocean, on a boat leaving India, and the scattering of memories and images as *maya*, illusion: "The signs are erased/ I watch clarity." (The third part of *East Slope* is the extremely complex triple-columned poem "Blanco," which, because of its length and format, could not be reproduced here. It may be found—along with other poems from India and the Spanish texts—in the New Directions edition of *Collected Poems 1957–1987*.)

In the ensuing years, references and allusions to India were omnipresent in Paz's work. He revisited the country in 1984 and 1985. But it was not until 1994 and 1995, in the months of convalescence following a serious operation, that his writing turned again directly to Indian traditions and his own experiences there. He published

a small book of adaptations of classical Sanskrit short poems (*kavya*), ten of which are included here. And he wrote *In Light of India*, a prose book that combines memoir, philosophical speculation, political analysis, history, and literary criticism, but which, he insists, like all his prose writing on India, is merely a footnote or gloss to the poems.

The German Romantics and the American Transcendentalists were obsessed with India, but never went. Eliot studied Sanskrit at Harvard, but lost interest later. Neruda lived for a while in Ceylon and hated it; Michaux merely passed through. Ginsberg and Snyder visited India, but their Buddhist commitments were to draw them, respectively, to the Tibetan diaspora and Japanese practice. No other Western poet has been as immersed in India as Paz. More incredibly, perhaps not since Victor Ségalen in China at the turn of the century has a Western poet been so expert on, experienced in, and written so extensively about, a cultural *other*. Our literary news of the world, for no reason, tends to come from novelists.

Again and again, Paz's poems return to two gardens: the one from his childhood in Mixcoac and the one he shared with Marie-José in India. Like everything in his work they are opposites, complements, mirrors facing each other with the poet, mid-ocean, adrift, in passage in-between. Sensual and illusory, they are unreal gardens full of real trees.

—Eliot Weinberger

11

I. MUTRA

.

MUTRA

Like a too-loving mother, a terrible mother of suffoca-
tion,
like a silent lioness of sunlight,
a single wave the size of the sea,
it has arrived noiselessly and in each of us has taken its
place like a king
and the glass days melt and in each breast is erected a
throne of thorns and live coals
and its dominion is a solemn hiccup, a crushed breathing of gods and animals with eyes dilated
and mouths full of hot insects uttering one same syllable
day and night, day and night.
Summer, enormous mouth, vowel made of fumes and
panting!

This day wounded to death creeping along the length of
time and never finished with dying,
and the day to come, now scraping impatiently at the
no-man's-land of dawn,
and the rest waiting their hour in the vast stables of the
year,
this day and its four pups, morning with its crystal tail
and noon with its one eye,
noon absorbed in its light, seated in splendor,
afternoon rich in birds, night with its bright stars armed
and in full regalia,
this day and the presences that the sun exalts or pulls
down with a simple wingblow:
the girl who appears in the street and is a stream of quiet
freshness,

the beggar raising himself up like a feeble prayer, a heap of garbage and whining canticles,

red bougainvillea black through darkness of red, purple in accumulated blue,

women bricklayers carrying stones on their heads as if they carried extinguished suns,

the beauty in her cave of stalactites, the sound of her scorpion's scales,

the man covered with ashes who worships the phallus, dung and water,

musicians who tear sparks out of daybreak and make the airy tempest of the dance come down to earth,

the collar of sparkle, electric garlands in equilibrium at midnight,

the sleepless children picking fleas by moonlight,

fathers and mothers with their family flocks and their beasts asleep and their gods petrified a thousand years ago,

butterflies, vultures, snakes, monkeys, cows, insects looking like madness,

all this long day with its frightful cargo of beings and things slowly being stranded on suspended time.

We all go declining with the day, we all enter the tunnel,

we cross through endless galleries whose walls of solid air close behind us,

we imprison ourselves in ourselves and at each step the human animal pants and topples,

we fall back, we give our ground, the animal loses the future at each step,

that which is erect and hard and bony in ourselves finally gives way, falling heavily into the mother mouth.

Within myself I crowd myself, in my own self I press
    myself and as I crowd myself I overflow,
I am extended and I expand, the full one, spilling and
    filling myself,
there is no vertigo nor mirror nor nausea facing the mir-
    ror, there is no downfall,
only a being, an overflowing being, full to the brim, and
    adrift:
not like the bow that curves and arches on itself to let the
    arrow leap straight to the mark,
not like the breast that awaits it, on whom hope already
    draws the wound,
not concentrated nor in trance, but tumbling from step
    to step, spilled water, we return to the origin.
And the head falls on the breast and body falls on body
    without finding its goal, its final body.

No, take hold of the ancient image: anchor existence and
    plant it in the stone, base of the lightning!
Some stones never give way, stones made of time, time
    made of stone, centuries that are columns,
assemblies singing the hymns of stone,
fountains of jade, obsidian gardens, towers of marble,
    high beauty armed against time.
One day my hand brushed against all that constructed
    glory.
Stones also lose their footing, stones too are images,
and they fall and they scatter and mix and flow with the
    flowing river.
The stones also are the river.
Where is the man who gives life to the stones of the dead,
    the man who makes the stones and the dead speak?

Foundations of stone and of music,
the factory that produces the mirrors of discourse and
   the poem's castle of fire
entwine their roots in his breast, rest in his head; his
   hand sustains them.
Under the breastplate of rock-crystal I searched for the
   man, groped for the imperceptible opening;
we are born and the rent is no more than a scratch and it
   never scars over and it burns and it is a star giving off
   its own light,
the little wound never quenched, the sign of the blood
   never erased, through that door we go down to the
   dark.
Man also flows, man also falls and is an image that van-
   ishes.

Marshes of lethargy, accretions of algae, bees in cata-
   racts over half-open eyes,
a feast of sand, hours chewed, images chewed, life
   chewed centuries
with no existence other than ecstatic chaos which floats
   among the sleeping waters,
water of eyes, water of mouths, wedding waters lost in
   contemplation, water of incest,
water of gods, copulation of gods, water of stars and
   reptiles, water-forests of burnt bodies,
beatitude of fullness, overflowing itself, we are not, I do
   not want to be
God, I do not want to grope in the dark, I will not return,
   I am a man and man is
man, he who leapt to the void and since then nothing
   has sustained him but his own wing,

the one who let go of his mother, the exiled, rootless,
   with neither heaven nor earth, a bridge, a bow
stretched over nothing, in himself unified, made whole,
   and nevertheless split from the moment of his birth,
   struggling
against his shadow, always running behind himself,
   blundering, exhausted, without ever reaching himself,
condemned from childhood, alembic of time, king of
   himself, son of his own works.

The ultimate images overthrown, the black river drowns
   consciousness,
night doubles over, the soul gives way, clusters of con-
   founded hours fall, man falls
like a star, the clusters of stars fall, like overripe fruit the
   world and its suns fall.
But in my head keep vigil adolescence and its images,
   the only treasure not ravaged:
ships afire on seas still unnamed and each wave striking
   memory in a storm of reminders
(fresh water in the island cisterns, fresh water of women
   and their voices sounding through the night like many
   streams meeting,
goddess of green eyes and human words who planted in
   our breast her reasons, a lovely procession of lances,
the calm reflection before a sphere, swollen with itself
   like an ear of wheat, but immortal, perfect, sufficient,
contemplation of numbers that join like notes or lovers,
the universe like a lyre, a bow, the victorious geometry
   of gods, sole abode that is worthy of man!)
and the high-walled city that on the plain glitters like a
   jewel in pain

and demolished watch-towers and the champion de-
feated and in the smoking chambers the treasure of
women
and the hero's epitaph stuck in the road at the narrow
place like a sword
and the poem rising and covering with its wings the
embrace of day and night
and the straight tree of discourse planted in potency in
the middle of the city
and justice in the open air of a people who weighs each
act in the scale of a delicate spirit sensitive to the
weight of light;
acts, the high pyres burnt by history!
Under these black remains asleep, truth, who roused the
works: man is only man among men.

And I reach down and grasp the incandescent grain and
plant it in my being: it must grow one day.

Delhi, 1952

II. EAST SLOPE

THE BALCONY

Stillness
in the middle of the night
not adrift with centuries
not spreading out
                    nailed
like a fixed idea
to the center of incandescence
Delhi
        Two tall syllables
surrounded by insomnia and sand
I say them in a low voice

                            Nothing moves
the hour grows
                    stretching out
It's summer
tide that spills over
I hear the low sky vibrate
over lethargic plains
Great masses obscene conclaves
clouds full of insects
flatten
        the vague dwarfed bulks
(Tomorrow they'll have names
they'll stand up and be houses
tomorrow they'll be trees)

Nothing moves
The hour is larger
         and I more alone
nailed
      to the center of the whirlwind
If I stretch out my hand
the air is a spongy body
a promiscuous faceless being
Leaning over the balcony
               I see

(*Never lean on a balcony
when you're alone,*
the Chinese poet writes)

It is not height nor the night and its moon
it is not the infinities that can be seen
but memory and its vertigoes
This that I see
         this spinning
is the tricks and traps
behind it there is nothing
it is the whirlwind of days
(Throne of bone
         throne of noon
that island
        On its lion-colored cliffs
I saw for an instant true life
It had the face of death
the same face
        dissolved
in the same sparkling sea)

What you have lived you will unlive today
you are not there
                              but here
I am here
                    at my beginning
I don't deny myself
                              I sustain myself
Leaning over the balcony
                              I see
huge clouds and a piece of the moon
all that is visible here
people houses
                    the real present
conquered by the hour
                              and all the invisible
here
        my horizon
If this beginning is a beginning
it does not begin with me
                              I begin with it
I perpetuate myself in it

                              Leaning over the balcony
I see
        this distance that is so close
I don't know what to call it
though I touch it with my thoughts
The night founders
the city like a mountain fallen
white lights blues yellows
sudden headlights walls of disgrace
and the terrible clusters

the clumps of people and animals on the ground
and the bramble of their tangled dreams

Old Delhi fetid Delhi
alleys and little squares and mosques
like a stabbed body
like a buried garden
For centuries it has rained dust
your veil is a dust-cloud
your pillow a broken brick
On a fig leaf
you eat the leftovers of your gods
your temples are bordellos of the incurable
you are covered with ants
abandoned lot
          ruined mausoleum
you are naked
          like a violated corpse
they stole your jewels and your burial clothes
You were covered with poems
your whole body was writing
remember
          recover the words
you are beautiful
          you know how to talk and sing and dance

Delhi
      two towers
planted on the plains
          two tall syllables
I say them in a low voice
leaning over the balcony
          nailed

not to the ground
                    to its vertigo
to the center of incandescence
I was there
              I don't know where
I am here
              I don't know is where
Not the earth
                    time
holds me in its empty hands
Night and moon
                    movements of clouds
tremor of trees
                    stupor of space
infinity and violence in the air
furious dust that wakes
The lights are on at the airport
murmur of song from the Red Fort
Distances
            a pilgrim's steps are vagabond music
on this fragile bridge of words
The hour lifts me
time hungers for incarnation
Beyond myself
                    somewhere
I wait for my arrival

THE TOMB OF AMIR KHUSRU
for Margarita and Antonio Gónzalez de León

Trees heavy with birds hold
the afternoon up with their hands.

Arches and patios. A tank of water,
poison green, between red walls.
A corridor leads to the sanctuary:
beggars, flowers, leprosy, marble.

Tombs, two names, their stories:
Nizam Uddin, the wandering theologian,
Amir Khusru, the parrot's tongue.
The saint and the poet. A grim
star sprouts from a cupola.
Slime sparkles in the pool.

Amir Khusru, parrot or mockingbird:
the two halves of each moment,
muddy sorrow, voice of light.
Syllables, wandering fires,
vagabond architectures:
each poem is time, and it burns.

THE RELIGIOUS FIG

Wind,
        the fruit thieves
(monkeys, birds, and bats)
scatter seeds
from the branches of the great tree.
Green, humming,
                        its entrails in the air,
it is a huge overflowing cup
where the suns drink.

                    The seeds
open,
        the plant encamps
on the void,
                    spins its vertigo
and within it grows tall and sways and spreads.
Years and years fall
                        in a straight line.
Its fall
        is a leap of water
frozen in its leap: petrified time.

It gropes its way,
                    sends out huge roots,
sinuous limbs,
                entangled
black jets,
            it sinks
pillars,
        excavates damp galleries
where echoes flare up and die,
copper vibration
                    resolved in the stillness
of a sun carbonized each day.
Arms, ropes, rings,
                    tangle
of masts and cables, a sloop run aground.

Creeping up,
                the wandering roots
entwine.

It is a bramble of hands.
They are not seeking earth: they seek a body,
weave into an embrace.
                              The tree
immures itself alive.
                              Its trunk
takes a hundred years to rot.
                              Its crown:
the bleached skull, the broken antlers of a deer.

Under a cape of leathery leaves,
a rippling that sings
                          from pink to gold to green,
knotted in itself,
                    two thousand years,
the fig tree creeps, rises up, and strangles itself.

THE MAUSOLEUM OF HUMAYUN

To the debate of wasps
the dialectic of monkeys
twitterings of statistics
it opposes
              (high flame of rose
formed out of stone and air and birds
time in repose above the water)

silence's architecture

IN THE LODI GARDENS
for Claude Esteban

The black, pensive, dense
domes of the mausoleums
suddenly shot birds
into the unanimous blue

THE DAY IN UDAIPUR

White palace,
white on the black lake.
Lingam and yoni.

        As the goddess to the god,
        you surround me, night.

Cool terrace.
You are immense, immense—
made to measure.

        Inhuman stars.
        But this hour is ours.

I fall and rise,
I burn, drenched.
Are you only one body?

        Birds on the water,
        dawn on eyelids.

Self-absorbed,
high as death,
the marble bursts.

               Hushed palaces,
               whiteness adrift.

Women and children
on the roads:
scattered fruit.

               Rags or rays of lightning?
               A procession on the plain.

Silver running cool
and clanking:
ankle and wrist.

               In a rented costume
               the boy goes to his wedding.

Clean clothes
spread out on the rocks
Look at them and say nothing.

               On the little island
               monkeys with red asses screech.

Hanging from the wall,
a dark and angry sun:
wasps' nest.

And my head is another sun,
full of black thoughts.

Flies and blood.
A small goat skips
in Kali's court.

Gods, men and beasts
eat from the same plate.

Over the pale god
the black goddess dances,
decapitated.

Heat, the hour split open,
and those mangoes, rotten . . .

Your face, the lake:
smooth, without thoughts.
A trout leaps.

Lights on the water:
souls sailing.

Ripples:
the golden plain—and the crack . . .
Your clothes nearby.

I, like a lamp
on your shadow body.

A living scales:
bodies entwined
over the void.

        The sky crushes us,
        the water sustains us.

I open my eyes:
so many trees
were born tonight.

        What I've seen here, what I say,
        the white sun erases.

THE OTHER

He invented a face for himself.
                     Behind it,
he lived died and was reborn
many times.
        His face now
has the wrinkles from that face.
His wrinkles have no face.

PERPETUA ENCARNADA

(*perpetually incarnadine:* the globe amaranth)

Intricate gardens tremble
the trees lean together
and whisper
        Day

is still burning in my eyes
Hour by hour I watched it slip away
wide and happy as a river
its banks twining shadow and light
and a yellow whirlwind
a single monotonous intensity
the sun fixed to its center
                              Gravitations
oscillations of impalpable matter
white demolitions
congregations of nomadic foam
great mountains up there
hanging from the light
unmoving glory smashed
by a blink
                    And down here
papayas mangoes tamarinds laurels
Norfolk Island pines cherimoyas
and the banyan
                        more forest than tree
green babble of millions of leaves
black fruit the pulsing sacks
of sleeping bats hanging from the branches

Everything was unreal in its excess

On the whitewashed wall
a play written by the wind and light
the shadows of the vines
greener than the word March
the mask of the afternoon
absorbed in the calligraphy of birds
Between the quivering grates of reflections

a transparent lizard
                        came and went
Insolent witty midget
changing places but not time
darting up and down through a now
with no before or after
                        From my own present tense
like one peering over a cliff
I watched it
            Sea-sickness
                        a swarming and a void
the afternoon the little beast my conscience
a vibration identical indifferent
And I saw in the white lime a purple explosion
so many suns in the blink of an eye
So much whiteness that it hurt

I sought asylum in the eucalypti
I begged for their shade
                        rain or thunder
always the same
                silence of roots
and the airy conversation of the leaves
I begged for moderation begged for perserverance
I am tied to time
                captured enraptured
I am in love with this world
I stumble lost in my self
craving wholeness craving indifference
to open my eyes
                impeccable evidence
among the clarities that dispute it

Not the abolition of images
the incarnation of pronouns
the world we invent among us
a community of signs
                    and at its center
the recluse
            Perpetua encarnada
half woman
                half spring in the rocks

Everyone's words that each says to himself
I begged that they would always be with me
human reason
the animal with radiant hands
the animal with eyes in its fingertips

The night gathers and expands
a knot of time a cluster of space
I see I hear I breathe
I beg for obedience to this day and night

ON THE ROADS OF MYSORE

Blue rocks, ruddy plains,
purple stony ground, clusters of cacti,
magueys, hacked forests—and the people:
is their skin darker or are their shawls whiter?
Hawk country, skies stretched
across wide-open land,
a land good for dreaming and riding horses.
In spite of the famines, the women are well-endowed:

full breasts and hips, jeweled and barefoot,
dressed in dazzling turquoise and magenta.
The men and women are tattooed.
A race of enormous eyes, stony gazes.
They speak gibberish, have strange rites,
but Tipu Sultan, the Tiger of Mysore,
is worth as much as Nayarit and its Tiger of Alica.

OOTACAMUND

1

In the Nilgiri Hills
I went looking for the Todas.
Their temples are cone-shaped and are stables.
Thin, bearded, impenetrable,
they milk their sacred buffaloes
murmuring incoherent hymns.
They guard a secret from Sumeria,
not knowing that they guard it.
Between the thin, dry lips of the elders
the name of Ishtar, the cruel goddess,
shines like the moon on an empty well.

2

On the verandah of the Cecil Hotel,
Miss Penelope (canary-colored hair,
woolen stockings and walking stick) has been saying
for thirty years: *Oh India,*
country of missed opportunities . . .
Above,
in the fireworks

of the jacaranda,
                    the crows
happily cackle.

3

Tall grass and low trees.
Uncertain ground. In the clearings
the winged termites construct
tiny Cyclopean castles.
Homages in sand
to Mycenae and Machu-Picchu.

4

Leafier and more brilliant,
the neem is like an ash:
a singing tree.

5

A vision on the mountain road:
the rose camelia tree
bending over the cliff.
Splendor in the sullen green,
fixed above an abyss.
Impenetrable presence,
indifferent to vertigo—and language.

6

The sky grows in the night,
eucalyptus set aflame.
The charitable stars
not crushing—calling me.

THE EFFECTS OF BAPTISM

Young Hassan,
in order to marry a Christian,
was baptized.
         The priest
named him Erik,
as though he were a Viking.
                  Now

he has two names
but only one wife.

COCHIN

1

Standing on tiptoe
to watch us go by,
among the coco-palms
tiny and white,
the Portuguese church.

2

Cinammon-colored sails.
The wind picks up:
breasts in breath.

3

With shawls of foam,
jasmine in their hair
and earrings of gold,

they go off to six o'clock mass
not in Mexico City or Cádiz:
in Travancore.

4

Beating more furiously
before the Nestorian patriarch:
my heretical heart.

5

In the Christian cemetery graze
dogmatic
                probably Shivaite
cows.

6

The same eyes see, the same afternoon:
the bougainvillaea with its thousand arms,
elephantiasis with its violet legs,
between the pink sea and the jaundiced palms.

MADURAI

In the bar at the British Club
—soft drinks, no Englishmen—
Our city is holy and rates high

                        he told me,
sucking up the last of his orangeade,
with the largest temple in India
(Minakshi, cinnamon goddess:)
and the T.S.V. Garage,

                    (your eyes are two fishes)
also the biggest in the subcontinent:
Sri K. J. Chidambaram,
I am connected with both institutions.
Director of The Great Lingam Inc.,
a bus company specializing in tourists.

HAPPINESS IN HERAT
for Carlos Pellicer

I came here
as I write these lines,
with no fixed idea:
a blue and green mosque,
six truncated minarets,
two or three tombs,
memories of a poet-saint,
the names of Timur and his line.
I met the wind of the hundred days.
It covered all the nights with sand,
badgered my forehead, scorched my lids.
Daybreak:
              scattering of birds
and that murmur of water on stones:
the footsteps of peasants.
(But the water tasted like dust.)
Whispers on the plains,
appearances
                disappearances,
golden whirlwinds
insubstantial as my thoughts.
Turning and turning

in a hotel room or in the hills:
the land a graveyard of camels
and in my quarrels always
the same crumbling faces.
Is the wind, lord of ruins,
my only master?
Erosions:
less grows more and more.

At the saint's tomb,
I drove a nail
deep into the dry tree,
                              not
like the others, against the evil eye:
against myself.
                    (I said something:
words the wind carried away.)

One afternoon the heights made a pact.
The poplars walked
                        going nowhere.
Sun on the tiles
                    sudden springs.
In the Ladies' Garden
I climbed to the turquoise cupola.
Minarets tattooed with signs:
the Cufic scripts, beyond letters,
became transparent.
I did not have the imageless vision,
I did not see forms whirl until they vanished
in unmoving clarity,
the being without substance of the Sufis.
I did not drink the plenitude of the void,

nor see the thirty-two marks
of the Boddhisattva's diamond body.
I saw a blue sky and all the blues,
from white to green,
the spread fan of the poplars,
and on a pine, more air than bird,
a black and white mynah.
I saw the world resting on itself.
I saw the appearances.
And I named that half-hour:
The Perfection of the Finite.

THE TANGHI-GARU PASS
for E. Cioran

Slashed earth:
winter marked the land with its weapons,
spring was dressed in thorns.

Mountains of mica. Black goats.
Under their sleepwalking hooves
the slate glitters, and is grim.

Fixed sun, nailed
to the enormous scar of stone.
Death thinks us.

SHARJ TEPE
for Pierre Dhainaut

Like a lion sprawled,
the same irritated color
of hairless hide:
                    the starving hill.
Across its ribs of earth,
                    arranged
in inexplicable order,
crude heaps of stones:
the cemetery of the White Huns.
Once in a while,
                    a sudden blue flap:
a bird,
        the only extravagance
amidst so much death.

APPARITION

If man is dust
those who go through the plain
are men

VILLAGE

The stones are time
                    The wind
centuries of wind
                    The trees are time
the people are stone

                    The wind
turns upon itself and sinks
into the stone day

There is no water here for all the luster of its eyes

HIMACHAL PRADESH (1)
for Juan Liscano

I saw
at the foot of the ridge
horizons undone
(In the skull of a horse
a hive of diligent bees)

I saw
vertigo petrified
the hanging gardens of asphyxia
(A tiger butterfly
motionless on the tip of a scent)

I saw
the mountains of the sages
where the wind mangles eagles
(A girl and an old woman, skin and bones
carry bundles bigger than these peaks)

THE FACE AND THE WIND

Beneath an unrelenting sun:
ocher plains, lion-colored hills.
I struggled up a craggy slope of goats

to a place of rubble:
lopped columns, headless gods.
Surreptitious flashes of light:
a snake, or some small lizard.
Hidden in the rocks,
the color of toxic ink,
colonies of brittle beetles.
A circular courtyard, a wall full of cracks.
Clutching the earth—blind knot,
tree all roots—a pipal, the religious fig.
Rain of light. A grey hulk: the Buddha,
its features a blurred mass.
Ants climbed and descended
the slopes of its face.
Still intact,
the smile, that smile:
a gulf of pacific clarity.
And I was, for a moment, diaphanous,
a wind that stops
turns on itself and is gone.

TOMB OF THE POET

The book
        the glass
the green obscurely a stalk
                        the record
sleeping beauty in her bed of music
things drowned in their names
to say them with the eyes
                        in a beyond I cannot tell where
nail them down

                    lamp pencil portrait
this that I see
                to nail it down

like a living temple
                        plant it
like a tree
            a god
crown it
        with a name
                        immortal
derisible crown of thorns
                        Speech!

The stalk and its imminent flower
                            sun-sex-sun
the flower without shadow
                        the word
opens
        in a beyond without where
immaculate extension
transparency which sustains things
fallen
        raised up
by the glance
                held
                    in a reflection

Bundle of worlds
                    instants
glowing bunches
moving forests of stars
wandering syllables

                              tide
all the times of time
                    TO BE
a second's fraction
                              lamp pencil portrait
in a here I cannot tell where

                              A name
begins
          seize on it, plant, say it
like a wood that thinks
                              flesh it
A lineage begins
                    in a name
an adam
              like a living temple
name without shadow
                              nailed
like a god
              in this here-without-where
Speech!

          I cease in its beginning
in this that I say
                    I cease
TO BE
          shadow of an instantaneous name

I SHALL NEVER KNOW MY BOND'S UNDOING

DAYBREAK

Hands and lips of wind
heart of water
     eucalyptus
campground of the clouds
the life that is born every day
the death that is born every life

I rub my eyes:
the sky walks the land

NIGHTFALL

What sustains it,
half-open, the clarity of nightfall,
the light let loose in the gardens?
All the branches,
conquered by the weight of birds,
lean toward the darkness.

Pure, self-absorbed moments
still gleam
on the fences.

Receiving night,
the groves become
hushed fountains.

A bird falls,
the grass grows dark,

edges blur, lime is black,
the world is less credible.

EXCLAMATION

Stillness
                not on the branch
in the air
                Not in the air
in the moment
                hummingbird

DISTANT NEIGHBOR

Last night an ash tree
was about to tell
me something—and didn't.

VRINDABAN

Surrounded by night
immense forest of breathing
vast impalpable curtains
murmurs
                I write
I stop
        I write

                    (All is and is not
and it all falls apart on the page
in silence)

                    A moment ago
a car raced down the street
among the extinguished houses
                              I raced
among my lighted thoughts
Above me the stars
                        such quiet gardens
I was a tree and spoke
was covered with leaves and eyes
was the rumor pushing forward
a swarm of images

(I set down now a few
twisted strokes
                    black on white
diminutive garden of letters
planted in the lamp's light)

The car raced on
through the sleeping suburb
                              I raced
to follow my thoughts
                          mine and others
Reminiscences leftovers imaginings
names
            The remains of sparks
            the laughter of the late parties
            the dance of the hours
            the march of the constellations

and other commonplaces
Do I believe in man
                        or in the stars?
I believe
          (with here a series
of dots)
          I see

A portico of weather-eaten pillars
statues carved by the plague
a double line of beggars
                        and the stench
a king on his throne
                    surrounded
by a coming and going of aromas
as if they were concubines
pure almost corporeal undulating
from the sandalwood to the jasmine
and its phantoms
Putrefaction
            fever of forms
                                fever of time
ecstatic in its combinations
The whole universe a peacock's tail
myriads of eyes
                    other eyes reflecting
modulations
            reverberations of a single eye
a solitary sun
                hidden
behind its cloth of transparencies
its tide of marvels
Everything was flaming

                    stones women water
Everything sculptured
                    from color to form
from form to fire
                    Everything was vanishing
Music of wood and metal
in the cell of the god
                    womb of the temple
Music
like the wind and water embracing
and over the entwined sounds
the human voice
a moon in heat at midday
stela of the disembodied soul

(I write without knowing the outcome
of what I write
                    I look between the lines
My image is the lamp
                    lit
in the middle of the night)

                    Mountebank
ape of the Absolute
                    cowering
pothook
        covered with pale ashes
a saddhu looked at me and laughed
watching me from the other shore
                                far off, far off
watching me like the animals like the saints
Naked   uncombed   smeared

a fixed ray a mineral glitter his eyes
I wanted to speak to him
he answered with a rumble of bowels

                                        Gone   gone
Where?
            To what region of being
to what existence
                        in the open air of what worlds
in what time?

                    (I write
each letter is a germ
                        The memory
imposes its tide
and repeats its own midday)

Gone   gone
                Saint   scoundrel   saint
in beatitudes of hunger or drugs
Perhaps he saw Krishna
                                    sparkling blue tree
dark fountain splashing amid the drought
Perhaps in a cleft stone
he grasped the form of woman
                                    its rent
the formless dizziness
                        For this or that
he lives on the ghat where they burn the dead

The lonely streets
the houses and their shadows
All was the same and all different

The car raced on
                    I was quiet
among my runaway thoughts

(Gone   gone
Saint   clown   saint   beggar   king   damned
it is the same
                    always the same
                                        within the same
It is to be always within oneself
closed up in the same
                    Closed up in oneself
rotted idol)

            Gone   gone
he watched me from the other shore
                                        he watches me
from his interminable noon
I am in the wandering hour
The car races on among the houses
I write by the light of a lamp
The absolutes the eternities
their outlying districts
                    are not my theme
I am hungry for life and for death also
I know what I know and I write it
The embodiment of time
                    the act
the movement in which the whole being
is sculptured and destroyed
Consciousness and hands to grasp the hour
I am a history

                    a memory inventing itself
I am never alone
I speak with you always
                              you speak with me always
I move in the dark
                    I plant signs

RELEASE
for Cintio Vitier

In a rain of drums
the flute's black stalk
grew, withered, and sprouted again
Things cast off from their names
I flowed
              at my body's edge
among the unbound elements

CONCERT IN THE GARDEN
(Vina and Mridangam)
for Carmen Figueroa de Meyer

It rained.
The hour is an enormous eye.
Inside it, we come and go like reflections.
The river of music
enters my blood.
If I say *body*, it answers *wind*.
If I say *earth*, it answers *where*?

The world, a double blossom, opens:
sadness of having come,
joy of being here.

I walk lost in my own center.

WRITING

I draw these letters
as the day draws its images
and blows over them

                  and does not return

CONCORD
for Carlos Fuentes

Water above
Grove below
Wind on the roads

Quiet well
Bucket's black   Spring water

Water coming down to the trees
Sky rising to the lips

SUNYATA

At the limits
          tinder

of charred space
the tree's
yellow ascension
                    Agate whirlwind
presence consumed
in a weightless glory
Hour after hour unleaving
the day
            now nothing
but a stalk
                of scattering vibrations
And amid such
                    indifferent bliss
it sprouts
            identical intact
the day
        The same that flows
through my hands
                        the same
ember on my eyelids
The day   The tree

YOUTH

The leap of the wave
                        whiter
each hour
            greener
each day
                younger
death

KAVYA: 10 EPIGRAMS FROM THE SANSKRIT

1

APPARITION ON THE RIVERBANK

She shakes her hair
and in the chaos of her curls
bright drops shine.
She crosses her arms and studies
the growing freshness of her breasts.
A cloth clings, translucent, to her thighs.
Bending slightly, with a quick glance
toward the bank, she comes out of the water.

—Bhojya-Deva

2

FIRST MEETING

Desire pushes her toward the encounter,
mistrust holds her back;
a silken banner, fluttering, limp,
furling and unfurling in the wind.

3

CONFIDENCE: CONFUSION

At the side of the bed
the knot came undone by itself,

and barely held by the sash
the robe slipped to my waist.
My friend, it's all I know: I was in his arms
and I can't remember who was who
or what we did or how.

—Vikatanitambā

4

THE SEAL

When will I see again her strong full thighs,
defensively closed, one against the other,
then opening, obedient to desire,
and as the silks slipped off, suddenly revealing,
like a wax seal on a secret treasure,
the marks, still moist, of my nails.

—Kishitisa

5

THE OBLIQUE INVITATION

Traveler, hurry your steps, be on your way:
the woods are full of wild animals,
snakes, elephants, tigers, and boars,
the sun's going down and you're so young to be going
    alone.
I can't let you stay,
for I'm a young girl and no one's home.

6

THE PEDAGOGUE

I wear no bracelets
golden as the autumn moon;
I've never known the taste of the lips
of a timid and tender young girl;
I have never won, by sword or pen,
fame in the halls of time:
I wasted my life in broken-down colleges,
teaching insolent, malicious boys.

7

WITHOUT FANFARE

It neither thunders nor hails,
shoots no lightning bolts,
nor unleashes great winds:
this huge cloud simply rains.

8

RHETORIC

Beauty is not
in what the words say
but in that which they say without saying it:
not naked, but through a veil,
breasts become desirable.

—Vallana

POSTERITY

Armed with their rules and precepts,
many condemn my verses.
I don't write for them,
but for that soul, twin to mine,
who will be born tomorrow.
Time is long and the world wide.

—Bhavabhūti

10

THE TRADITION

No one behind, no one ahead.
The path the ancients cleared has closed.
And the other path, everyone's path,
easy and wide, goes nowhere.
I am alone and find my way.

—Dharmakīrti

III. TOWARD THE BEGINNING

WIND FROM ALL COMPASS POINTS

The present is motionless
The mountains are of bone and of snow
they have been here since the beginning
The wind has just been born
                           ageless
as the light and the dust
                          A windmill of sounds
the bazaar spins its colors
                    bells   motors   radios
the stony trot of dark donkeys
songs and complaints entangled
among the beards of the merchants
the tall light chiseled with hammer-strokes
In the clearings of silence
                    boys' cries
     explode
Princes in tattered clothes
on the banks of the tortured river
pray   pee   meditate

                           The present is motionless
The floodgates of the year open
                  day flashes out
          agate
     The fallen bird
between rue Montalambert and rue de Bac
is a girl
         held back

at the edge of a precipice of looks
If water is fire
                    flame
                            dazzled
in the center of the spherical hour
                    a sorrel filly
A marching battalion of sparks
                                    a real girl
among wraithlike houses and people
Presence a fountain of reality
I looked out through my own unrealities
I took her hand
                    together we crossed
the four quadrants the three times
floating tribes of reflections
and we returned to the day of beginning

The present is motionless
                            June 21st
today is the beginning of summer
                                    Two or three birds
invent a garden
                    You read and eat a peach
on the red couch
                    naked
like the wine in the glass pitcher
                                A great flock of crows
Our brothers are dying in Santo Domingo
"If we had the munitions
                            You people would not be here"
                    We chew our nails down to the elbow
In the gardens of his summer fortress

Tipu Sultan planted the Jacobin tree
then distributed glass shards among
the imprisoned English officers
and ordered them to cut their foreskins
and eat them
                    The century
has set fire to itself in our lands
Will the builders of cathedrals and pyramids
charred hands
                    raise their transparent houses
by its light?

                    The present is motionless
The sun has fallen asleep between your breasts
The red covering is black and heaves
Not planet and not jewel
                              fruit
you are named
                    date
                    Datia
castle of Leave-If-You-Can
                              scarlet stain
upon the obdurate stone
Corridors
              terraces
                        stairways
dismantled nuptial chambers
of the scorpion
                    Echoes repetitions
the intricate and erotic works of a watch
                                        beyond time
                                        You cross

taciturn patios under the pitiless afternoon
a cloak of needles on your untouched shoulders
If fire is water
                              you are a diaphanous drop
the real girl
                      transparency of the world

The present is motionless
                                        The mountains
                          quartered suns
petrified storm earth-yellow
                                        The wind whips
                                                          it hurts to see
The sky is another deeper abyss
                                        Gorge of the Salang Pass
black cloud over black rock
Fist of blood strikes
                          gates of stone
Only the water is human
in these precipitous solitudes
Only your eyes of human water
                                        Down there
in the cleft
desire covers you with its two black wings
Your eyes flash open and close
                                        phosphorescent animals
Down there
                  the hot canyon
the wave that stretches and breaks
                                        your legs apart
the plunging whiteness
the foam of our bodies abandoned

                              The present is motionless
The hermit watered the saint's tomb
his beard was whiter than the clouds
Facing the mulberry
                    on the flank of the rushing stream
you repeat my name
                        dispersion of syllables
A young man with green eyes presented you
with a pomegranate
                        On the other bank of the Amu-Darya
smoke rose from Russian cottages
The sound of an Usbek flute
was another river invisible clearer
The boatman
                  on the barge was strangling chickens
The countryside is an open hand
                              its lines
                  marks of a broken alphabet
Cow skeletons on the prairie
Bactria
        a shattered statue
I scraped a few names out of the dust
By these fallen syllables
seeds of a charred pomegranate
I swear to be earth and wind
                              whirling
over your bones

                  The present is motionless
Night comes down with its trees
night of electric insects and silken beasts
night of grasses which cover the dead

meeting of waters which come from far off
rustlings
                    universes are strewn about
a world falls
                    a seed flares up
each word beats
                    I hear you throb in the shadow
a riddle shaped like an hourglass
                                        woman asleep
Space   living spaces
Anima mundi
                    maternal substance
always torn from itself
always falling into your empty womb
                                        Anima mundi
mother of the nomadic tribes
                            of suns and men
The spaces turn
                    the present is motionless

At the top of the world
Shiva and Parvati caress
                            Each caress lasts a century
for the god and for the man
                            an identical time
an equivalent hurling headlong
                            Lahore
                                        red river black boats
a barefoot girl
                    between two tamarinds
and her timeless gaze
                    An identical throbbing

72

death and birth
A group of poplars
suspended betwen sky and earth
they are a quiver of light more than a trembling of leaves
                    Do they rise
                                        or fall?

The present is motionless
                            It rains on my childhood
it rains on the feverish garden
flint flowers   trees of smoke
In a fig leaf you sail
                        on my brow
The rain does not wet you
you are flame of water
                            the diaphanous drop of fire
spilling upon my eyelids
I look out through my own unrealities
the same day is beginning
                            Space wheels
the world wrenches up its roots
Our bodies
            stretched out
                            weigh no more than dawn

MADRIGAL

More transparent
than this water dropping
through the vine's twined fingers
my thought stretches a bridge

from yourself to yourself
                              Look at you
more real than the body you inhabit
fixed at the center of my mind

You were born to live on an island

WITH EYES CLOSED

With eyes closed
you light up within
you are blind stone

Night after night I carve you
with eyes closed
you are frank stone

We have become enormous
just knowing each other
with eyes closed

PASSAGE

More than air
                    more than water
more than lips
                    lighter lighter

Your body is the trace of your body

WITH YOU

Turquoise blasts of wind
parrots in pairs flit by
                        Rages
the world flames
                    A tree
seething with crows
blazes and does not burn
                            Calm
amidst the tall sunflowers
                            you are
a pause of light
                The day
is a great clear word
a fluttering of vowels
                        Your breasts
ripen before my eyes
                        My thoughts
are lighter than the air
                            I am real
I see my life and death
The world is true
I see
        I inhabit a transparency

SUN ON A BLANKET

Riddled with light
                    half a wall
a vertical salt-pan

                    The curtain: spilled shadow
blue swell of the sea
                              over the lime of the other half
Outside the sun battles the sea
The tile floor
                    breathes is breathing
The blue stretches out
                              on the bed
A rose pillow props
                    a girl
Her red dress still warm
                              her eyes half-closed
not in waiting
                    in the visitation
She is barefoot
                    Unpolished silver wraps around
and cools
          her bare arm
The sun's dagger dances on her warrior breast
Toward her belly
                    eminent imminent
a line of black ants climb
She opens her eyes
                    from the burnt honey
black honey
                    to the poppy's glint
black light
                    A pitcher on a table
A sunflower above the pitcher
                              The girl
on the blue blanket
                    a cooler sun

MAITHUNA

My eyes discover you
naked
      and cover you
with a warm rain
of glances

                 *

A cage of sounds
                 open
to the morning
              whiter
than your thighs
             at night
your laughter
            and more your foliage
your blouse of the moon
                  as you leap from bed

Sifted light
           the singing spiral
spools whiteness
           Chiasm
X
  planted in a chasm

                 *

My day
        exploded
in your night
           Your shriek

leaps in pieces
                    Night
spreads
        your body
washing under
                    your bodies
knot
Your body once again

                              *

Vertical hour
                    drought
spins its flashing wheels
Garden of knives
                    feast of deceit
Through these reverberations
                              you enter
unscathed
        the river of my hands

                              *

Quicker than fever
you swim in darkness
                    your shadow clearer
between caresses
                    your body blacker
You leap
        to the bank of the improbable
toboggans of how when because yes
Your laughter burns your clothes
                              your laughter
soaks my forehead my eyes my reasons

Your body burns your shadow
You swing on a trapeze of fear
the terrors of your childhood
                              watch me
from your cliffhanging eyes
                              wide-open
making love
              at the cliff
Your body clearer
                    your shadow blacker
You laugh over your ashes

                    *

Burgundy tongue of the flayed sun
tongue that licks your land of sleepless dunes
hair unpinned
                    tongue of whips
                              spoken tongues
unfastened on your back
                          enlaced
on your breasts
                    writing that writes you
with spurred letters
                    denies you
with branded signs
                          dress that undresses you
writing that dresses you in riddles
writing in which I am buried
                              Hair unpinned
the great night swift over your body
jar of hot wine
              spilled

on the tablets of the law
knot of howling and cloud of silence
cluster of snakes
                    cluster of grapes
trampled
          by the cold soles of the moon
rain of hands leaves fingers wind
on your body
                on my body on your body
Hair unpinned
                foliage of the tree of bones
the tree of aerial roots that drink night from the sun
The tree of flesh   The tree of death

                          *

Last night
          in your bed
we were three:
the moon   you & me

                          *

I open
        the lips of your night
damp hollows
                unborn
echoes:

          whiteness
a rush
        of unchained water

To sleep to sleep in you
or even better to wake
                              to open my eyes
at your center
                    black white black
white
          To be the unsleeping sun
your memory ignites
                              (and
the memory of me in your memory

*

And again the sap skywise
rises
      (salvia your name
is flame)
              Sapling
crackling
              (rain
of blazing snow)
                        My tongue
is there
          (Your rose
burns through the snow)
                                    is
now
      (I seal your sex)
                              dawn
from danger drawn

THE ARMS OF SUMMER

Hear the throbbing of space
it is the steps of a season in heat
across the embers of the year

Murmur of wings and rattles
the far-off drumbeats of the storm
the crackling and panting of the earth
under its cape of roots and bugs

Thirst wakes and builds
great cages of glass
where your nakedness is water in chains
water that sings and breaks loose from its chains

Armed with the arms of summer
you come into my room come into my mind
and untie the river of language
look at yourself in these hurried words

Bit by bit the day burns out
over the erasing landscape
your shadow is a land of birds
the sun scatters with a wave

THE KEY OF WATER

After Rishikesh
the Ganges is still green.
The glass horizon

breaks among the peaks.
We walk upon crystals.
Above and below
great gulfs of calm.
In the blue spaces
white rocks, black clouds.
You said:
> *Le pays est plein de sources.*
That night I dipped my hands in your breasts.

AXIS

Through the conduits of blood
my body in your body
                spring of night
my tongue of sun in your forest
                        your body a kneading trough
I red wheat
           Through the conduits of bone
I night I water
              I forest that moves forward
I tongue
        I body
             I sun-bone
Through the conduits of night
                   spring of bodies
You night of wheat
              you forest in the sun
you waiting water
              you kneading trough of bones
Through the conduits of sun

                    my night in your night
my sun in your sun
                    my wheat in your kneading trough
your forest in my tongue
                    Through the conduits of the body
water in the night
                    your body in my body
Spring of bones
                    Spring of suns

ALTAR

                    A name
                  Its shadows
          He   She
          An i   An o
        A mallet   A gong
        A tower   A pool
        A hand   A clock
        A bone   A rose
        A mist   A tomb
        A spring   A flame
        A brand   A night
        A river   A city
        A keel   An anchor
                    She male
                      He
                  Body of names
    Your name in my name in your name my name
One to another one against the other one around another
                  One in the other
                    Unnamed

84

SUNDAY ON THE ISLAND OF ELEPHANTA

At the feet of the sublime sculptures,
vandalized by the Muslims and the Portuguese,
the crowds have left a picnic of garbage
for the crows and dogs.
I condemn them to be reborn a hundred times
on a dungheap,
                        and as for the others,
for eons they must carve living flesh
in the hell for the mutilators of statues.

INVOCATION

Shiva and Parvati:
                        we worship you
not as gods
            but as images
of the divinity of man.
You are what man makes and is not,
what man will be
when he has served the sentence of hard labor.
Shiva:
        your four arms are four rivers,
four jets of water.
                        Your whole being is a fountain
where the lovely Parvati bathes,
where she rocks like a graceful boat.
The sea beats beneath the sun:
it is the great lips of Shiva laughing;
the sea is ablaze:

it is the steps of Parvati on the waters.
Shiva and Parvati:
                        the woman who is my wife
and I
            ask you for nothing, nothing
that comes from the other world:
                                    only
the light on the sea,
the barefoot light on the sleeping land and sea.

A TALE OF TWO GARDENS

A house, a garden,
                    are not places:
they spin, they come and go.
                            Their apparations open
another space
                in space,
another time in time.
                        Their eclipses
are not abdications:
the vivacity of one of those moments
                                    would burn us
if it lasted a moment more.
                            We are condemned
to kill time:
                so we die,
little by little.
                    A garden is not a place.
Down a path of reddish sand,
we enter a drop of water,

drink green clarities from its center,
we climb
                the spiral of hours
to the tip of the day,
                        descend
to the last burning of its ember.
Mumbling river,
                the garden flows through the night.

That one in Mixcoac, abandoned,
covered with scars,
                        was a body
at the point of collapse.
                        I was a boy,
and the garden for me was like a grandfather.
I clambered up its leafy knees,
not knowing it was doomed.
The garden knew it:
                        it awaited its destruction
as a condemned man awaits the axe.
The fig tree was a goddess,
                        the Mother.
Hum of irascible insects,
the muffled drums of the blood,
the sun and its hammer,
the green hug of innumerable limbs.
The cleft in the trunk:
                        the world half-opened.
I thought I had seen death:
                        I saw
the other face of being,
                        the feminine void,
the fixed featureless splendor.

White leagues batter
the crest of Ajusco,
                    turn black,
a purple mass,
                    a great bulge splitting open:
the rainsquall's gallop covers the plain.
Rain on lava:
                the water dances
on bloodstained stone.
                        Light, light:
the stuff of time and its inventions.
Months like mirrors,
one by the other reflected and effaced.
Days when nothing happens,
studying an ants' nest,
its subterranean labor,
its fierce rites.
                    Immersed in the cruel light,
I washed my ants' nest body,
                        I watched
the restless construction of my ruin.
Elytra:
        the insect's razor song
slices the dry grass.
                    Mineral cacti,
quicksilver lizards in adobe walls,
the bird that drills through space,
thirst, tedium, clouds of dust,
impalpable epiphanies of wind.
The pines taught me to talk to myself.
In that garden I learned to wave myself goodbye.

Later there were no gardens.
                              One day,
as if I had returned,
                    not to my house,
but to the beginning of the Beginning,
                                   I reached a clarity.
Space made of air
                    for the passionate games
of water and light.
                    Diaphanous convergences:
from the twittering of green
                              to the most humid blue
to the grey of embers
                         to a woundlike pink
to an unburied gold.
                       I heard a dark green murmur
burst from the center of the night: the neem tree.
On its shoulders,
                    the sky
with all its barbarian jewels.
The heat was a huge closing hand,
one could hear the roots panting,
space expanding,
the crumbling of the year.
                            The tree would not give way.
Huge as a monument to patience,
fair as the balance that weighs
                              a dewdrop,
                              a grain of light,
                              an instant.
Many moons fit in its branches.
House of squirrels,
                    blackbird inn.

Strength is fidelity,
                    power reverence:
no one ends at himself,
                    each one is an all
in another all,
                    in another one.
The other is contained in the one,
                              the one is another:
we are constellations.
                    The enormous neem
once knew how to be small.
                              At its feet
I knew I was alive,
                    I knew
that death is expansion,
                    self-negation is growth.
I learned,
        in the brotherhood of the trees,
to reconcile myself,
                    not with myself:
with what lifts me, sustains me, lets me fall.

I crossed paths with a girl.
                    Her eyes:
the pact between the summer and the autumn suns.
She was a follower of acrobats, astronomers, camel drivers.
I of lighthouse keepers, logicians, saddhus.
                                    Our bodies
spoke, mingled, and went off.
We went off with them.
                    It was the monsoon.
Skies of grass-bits
                    and armed wind

at the crossroads.
                              I named her Almendrita
after the girl of the story,
sailor of a stormy pond.
                              Not a name:
an intrepid sailboat.
                              It rained,
the earth dressed and became naked,
snakes left their holes,
the moon was made of water,
                              the sun was water,
the sky took out its braids
and its braids were unraveled rivers,
the rivers swallowed villages,
death and life were jumbled,
dough of mud and sun,
season of lust and plague,
season of lightning on a sandalwood tree,
mutilated genital stars
                    rotting,
reviving in your womb,
                    mother India,
girl India,
drenched in semen, sap, poisons, juices.

Scales grew on the house.
                    Almendrita:
flame intact through the snaking and the wind-gust,
in the night of the banana leaves,
                              green ember,
hamadryad,
          yakshi:
                    laughter in the brambles,

bundle of brightness in the thicket,
                              more music
than body,
              more bird-flight than music,
more woman than bird:
                    your belly the sun,
sun in the water,
                    sun-water in the earthen jar,
sunflower seed I planted in my chest,
agate,
        ear of flame in the garden of bones.

For his funeral,
Chuang-tzu asked heaven for its lights,
                                    the wind for its cymbals.
We asked the neem to marry us.
A garden is not a place:
                    it is a passage,
a passion.
            We don't know where we're going,
to pass through is enough,
                        to pass through is to remain:
a dizzying immobility.
                    Seasons,
the waves of months.
                    Each winter
a terrace above the year.
                        Well-tempered light,
resonance, transparency,
                        sculptures of air
dissolved as soon as they are said:
                        syllables,

the fortunate isles!

                  A sneak in the grass,
Demosthenes the cat is a luminous coal;
the female, Semiramis, chases ghosts,

                               stalks

reflections, shadows, echoes.

                       Above,

the sarcastic crows;

                 the capercaillie and his mate,
exiled princes;

             the hoopoe,
crest and beak a fancy brooch;
the green artillery of the parakeets;
bats the color of nightfall.
On the fixed, empty,

                  even sky,

a kite

       draws and erases circles.
Now,

       silent

             on a wave's arista:

an albatross,

             a cliff of foam.
Sudden

          scatter into wings.
We're not far from Durban

                   (where Pessoa studied).

We pass a tanker,

             heading for Mombassa,
that port with the name of a fruit.

                    (In my blood:
Camoens, Vasco da Gama, and the rest . . .)

The garden has been left behind.

Behind or ahead?

There are no more gardens than those we carry within.
What waits for us on the other bank?
Passion is passage:

the other bank is here,

light in the bankless air,

Prajnaparamita,

Our Lady of the Other Bank,

you yourself,

the girl of the tale,

alumna of the garden.

I forgot Nagarjuna and Dharmakirti

in your breasts,

I found them in your cry,

Maithuna,

two in one,

one in all,

all in nothing,

sunyata,

the empty plenitude,

emptiness round as your hips!

Cormorants above
a rippling pool of light
fish for their shadows.

The vision scatters in a whirlwind,
helix of seventeen syllables

drawn on the sea,

not by Basho:

by my eyes, the sun and the birds,

today, at about four,
                              at the latitude of Mauritania.
A wave explodes:
                              salt butterflies.
Metamorphosis into the identical.
                              At this same moment,
Delhi and its red stones,
                              its muddy river,
its white domes,
                              its centuries in smithereens,
transform:
                              weightless structures,
almost mental crystallizations.
                              Dizziness,
vertigo high above a mirror.
                              The garden sinks.
Now it is a name with no substance.

The signs are erased:
                              I watch clarity

Author's Notes

[editor's notes in square brackets]

I. MUTRA

The city of Mutra (Mathura) was a great center of civilization in ancient India, and even today has an important function in the religious life of those who worship Krishna. It was settled in the 6th century B.C., and enjoyed a period of artistic, political, and commercial splendor under the rule of the Kushans, between the 1st and 4th centuries A.D. The Kushans were an Indo-European people from central Asia who burst into the history of the subcontinent in the time of the civil and dynastic wars that followed the disintegration of the Maurya empire. The first mention of the Kushans is in Chinese, in the chronicles of the Han dynasty, where they are called *yueh-chih,* and their tribal chiefs *kuei-shuang* (Kushans). Displaced by the other nomadic tribes that threatened the borders of the Han empire, the *yueh-chih* appeared on the banks of the Oxus River around the 2nd century B.C. They soon crossed the great river and took possession of Bactria, the rich land that had been ruled for a short and brilliant period by the successors of Alexander, and then had fallen under the dominion of the Sakas (Scythians). The Kushans quickly spread throughout what is present-day Afghanistan, and continued on to Taxila (which is celebrated in the annals of Buddhism, as well as in the history of the Bactrian Greeks), the Punjab and, finally, the Ganges valley. In a few years they were able to create a vast empire that lasted more than three centuries. The Kushans abandoned their barbaric past and successfully assimilated the cultures they encountered in their expansion: the Persians and the Indo-Greeks. Their great centers were Surkh Kotal in Afghanistan, of which only ruins remain; the famous Taxila in Pakistan,

which has left us memorable works and objects; and Mathura, which was the winter capital of the Kushan rulers. From that time on, Mathura was a celebrated city, and it frequently appeared in the annals, poems, and stories of classical India. For example, one of the most entertaining tales in Somadeva's *The Ocean of Story*, a picaresque account of the love of the beautiful courtesan Rupanika for a young Brahman, takes place there.

Situated on the right bank of the Yamuna River, which later joins the Ganges, Mathura has been the victim of successive invasions and sackings. The most powerful of these has been time, the great leveller. Scandalously, there has been no modern archeological excavation of either the city or its outskirts; surely under the cement of the present-day city and in the hills that surround it there are buried temples, palaces, and stupas. Among the invasions that Mathura has suffered in its two thousand years of history, the cruelest was that of Mahamud of Gazni who, in 1017, sacked the city and burned it to the ground, taking away objects and statues of silver and gold.

Despite all these catastrophes, Mathura today maintains a small but notable museum built in the last years of the English Viceroyalty, and still called the Curzon Museum of Archeology, in honor of the British statesman. Visiting this museum is gratifying: one can see the whole collection in little more than an hour, but almost every piece in it is extraordinary, especially the statues of the Buddha and the tree-spirits, the *yakshas* and their companions and consorts, the *yakshis*, the graceful and sensual nymphs of Hindu mythology. Almost all of these sculptures—except for a few pieces that are in the Gandhara Buddhist Greco-Roman style—are made of the red stone that is characteristic of the region. They display the features of classical (Gupta) Indian sculpture: the plenitude of forms, sensuality, majesty of proportions, a corporal energy that is never without a kind of softness, and even languidness in the lines. A predominance of curves and undulations. A carnal irradiation inhabited, one might say, by an indefinable spirituality. Statues that are of this world and of the next.

The great art of classical India begins with Mathura in the Kushan period and, contemporary to it, the Hellenistic sculptures of the Gandhara and the reaction to them. The Curzon Museum also contains pieces of a geometric style, both synthetic and rigid, that are probably Scythian. The most impressive of these is the colossal statue of the king Kanishka, the conqueror and ruler of an enormous empire. He is dressed as a warrior: heavy boots, a tunic, a cape, a huge sword, and a mace on which he rests his left hand. A living image of power. And yet, like a terrible warning from time itself about the immoderation of man, the statue has no head. Although its decapitation was an accident—the work of time or of grave-robbers—one can see it as a strange confirmation of one of the legends that surrounds his memory.

Kanishka reigned in the first century of our era (the exact dates are unknown) and it seems that he was an important protector of Buddhism. In the Buddhist chronicles and legends he is equal, as a sovereign, to the great Ashoka, the pious Maurya emperor. It is said that Kanishka convoked a huge council in Kashmir, built the great stupa of Peshawar (which is still unexcavated), and was the friend, admirer, and patron of the poet Ashavaghosa, who is venerated by all Buddhists as the author of, among other works, the poem *Buddhacarita,* which relates the legendary life of Sakyamuni.

According to the legend, Kanishka was a warrior and a conqueror, a man of the sword, blood, and violence, and at his death he deserved to go to hell. The pious Ashavaghosa saved him, and he was reborn as a fish with a thousand heads. To punish him for his violence, a gigantic knife cut off the heads of this enormous fish, one by one, until the tolling of a bell from a Buddhist monastery came across the waters. To alleviate the suffering of the king—another merciful act by Ashavaghosa—the bell did not cease to ring until Kanishka was born again. How many times, and in what forms and in which gender has he been reborn? Today he is perhaps an atomic physicist or a Hollywood star.

Besides its aesthetic and literary importance, Mathura is a holy city. Krishna was born there, and the nearby village of Vrindaban was the scene of his love for the cowgirl Radha, the subject of innumerable poems, songs, and miniatures. The region was heavily forested, as one can see in the miniatures, but today it is an arid plain. Thousands of pilgrims come to Mathura and Vrindaban to perform their ritual ablutions on the ghats of the Yamuna. (A ghat is a stairway of stone or rubblework that descends from the bank to the river.) The river is full of turtles. In one of the temples, they perform each night a beautiful ceremony: the priests light small candles that they launch on the river in tiny and fragile boats made of leaves, while, to the sound of cymbals, the Brahmans chant hymns to and feed the turtles.

I visited Mathura in the summer of 1952, shortly after my arrival in India. There, I was seduced by the statues of the *yakshis*, represented in graceful and lascivious postures; I trembled before the decapitated red sculpture of Kanishka; I watched the ceremony from a boat on the river: the songs of the priests, the little candles floating for a few minutes before being swallowed by the night, the turtles slowly rising to the banks of the Yamuna.

About my poem, I can say little—I feel remote from its language—except that, as I told Alfonso Reyes in a letter at the time, I wrote it to defend myself against the metaphysical temptation of India. In those days, I had just read some fragments of his translation of the *Iliad*; the allusions to Greece in the final stanza are an echo of that reading. "The subject of the poem," I wrote in a note years later, "is the arrival of summer in the city and the fevers it generates on the earth and in the mind. A subject associated with Hinduism and its search for unity in the plurality of the forms of life. The end of the poem sets against this metahistorical absolute the idea of life as action and heroism which we have inherited from the Greeks." In 1963, I visited Vrindaban, another holy place of Hinduism. I experienced a similar reaction and wrote another poem. Both poems are the instinctive and defensive expression of modern Western activism. A somewhat more balanced and just posi-

tion is taken in the final chapter of *In Light of India*. What the moderns have failed to undertake—as centuries of Indian thought once did—is a critique of time and of its senseless and ultimately illusory acceleration. We must make this critique on our own account, and from our own suppositions. We need to relearn the ancient and forgotten art of contemplation.

Mexico City, 10 July 1995

II. EAST SLOPE

[The title is an homage to the Sung Dynasty poet Su Shih (1037–1101), whose pen name was Su Tung-p'o, "East Slope."]

THE BALCONY
Chinese poet: Li Yu (937–978), the last Emperor of the Southern Tang Dynasty. The lines quoted are from a poem written in exile.
pilgrim's steps: the first line of Gongora's dedication to the *Soledades*.

THE TOMB OF AMIR KHUSRU
The sanctuary of Nizam Ud-din is in Delhi: a mosque, a water tank, and various tombs. The most important are those of the saint and of the poet. Nizam Ud-din was a Sufi theologian and mystic of the 14th century. His debate with Sultan Ghiryasun-in Tughluq is well-known (see the chronicles of Ibn Bahtuta). Amir Khusru, friend and disciple of Nizam Ud-din, was a poet and musician. Although of Afghan origin, he is considered the founder of Urdu poetry. On his tomb is an inscription in Persian, with this harsh praise: "the sweet-tongued parrot.'"

THE RELIGIOUS FIG
The tree in question is the pipal (*Ficus religiosus*), first cousin to the banyan (*Ficus benghalensis*). Both "commonly start life from seed deposited by birds, squirrels, monkeys or fruit-eating bats, high upon a palm or other native tree. The roots grow

downward, attached to the trunk of the supporting plant, but they are not parasitic. . . . The name *strangler* has become attached to fig trees which grow in this way, since their descending and encircling roots become at length largely or entirely confluent, forming a pseudo-trunk hollow at the center through which the dead or dying host tree passes. . . . Roots of fig trees often enter cracks and crevices, thus causing serious injury to buildings and walls on which they are growing" (*Encyclopedia Britannica*). The properties of these trees, as well as their longevity—they last for hundreds of years, and some, it is said, are contemporaries of the Buddha or of his immediate disciples—are even more disturbing than their scientific name: the religious fig. For Buddhists, the pipal is sacred, and it appears in their sculpture, paintings, poems, and religious tales. In its shade Gautama perceived the truth and became the Buddha, the Enlightened One; for this reason it is called the Tree of Enlightenment (*bo,* or *boddhi*). The pipal is also sacred to Hindus. It is associated with the Krishna cult; on its branches the god hung the clothes of the cowgirls who bathed in the Yamuna, a favorite subject of erotic poems and paintings. The pipal and the banyan are central elements of the Indian landscape: every hamlet has one, center for meeting and play, sanctuary of Hanuman, the monkey god, trysting-place for lovers, and witness to the visions of mystics.

THE MAUSOLEUM OF HUMAYUN
Son of Babur, conqueror of India, the emperor Humayun was the father of the great Akbar. The family descends from Timur or Tamerlan, Marlowe's Tamburlaine. Near the mausoleum there is, or used to be, one of those centers for the study of what economists and sociologists call "underdevelopment," bustling with Indian functionaries and foreign "experts."

IN THE LODI GARDENS
The mausoleums of the Lodi Dynasty (1451–1526) in Delhi.

THE DAY IN UDAIPUR

The palaces of Udaipur (Rajasthan) belong to the final phase of Indo-Saracen art, and are from the 17th and 18th centuries.

lingam: phallic symbol of the god Shiva.

yoni: sexual symbol of the great goddess.

In a rented costume: In the bazaar of Udaipur there is a shop where grooms—most of them boys from the peasant castes—rent the sumptuous costumes that tradition requires for the wedding ceremony.

in Kali's court: Small goats are sacrificed in the Kali temples. The meat of the decapitated animals is sold to the devout, and the rest given to beggars.

Over the pale god: Black Kali dances on the prone (dead or asleep) body of the ascetic Shiva, who is covered with ashes. In her frenzy she decapitates herself. (Cf. the interpretation of the myth in Heinrich Zimmer's *Myths and Symbols in Indian Art and Civilization.*)

PERPETUA ENCARNADA

The globe amaranth is an herbaceous plant whose flowers remain intact for months. In the poem: poetry.

banyan: the Bengal fig (*Ficus benghalensis*). On the "moeurs" of this tree, see above, the note on the religious fig. Banyans rise to a height of three or four meters and, owing to the profusion of their aerial roots, their diameter is enormous. A banyan seems more like many trees than one. It was named by European travelers after the merchants (*banyans*) who used to erect stalls in its shade.

ON THE ROADS OF MYSORE

Tipu Sultan: "The Tiger of Mysore," and the principal Mughal prince to fight, at the end of the 18th century, against the British in South India. Among his military and political advisers were various French officials. He founded the Jacobin Club of Mysore and was its first (and only) president.

Tiger of Alica: Antonio Losada, Mexican guerrilla of the 19th century.

There is an extensive anthropological literature on the Todas: their rites associated with the milking of sacred buffaloes, their kinship system, their oral poetry, and their supposed practice of child-sacrifice. Their origin is unknown. Some see them as descendants of a colony of Sumerian-Babylonian merchants who were unable to return to Mesopotamia on account of the Aryan invasions of the 2nd Millennium B.C. Advocates of this hypothesis, now doubted by many anthropologists, cite in their defense the prayers recited by the priests as they milk the sacred buffaloes, which contain, more or less distorted, the names of various Sumerian-Babylonian gods, among them the goddess Ishtar. The priests admit that these names are meaningless to them.

neem: (Azadirachta indica), an abundant shade tree. Its roots and bark are medicinal, its twigs are used for cleaning teeth. Like the pipal and the banyan, the neem appears in the folk poetry, but it is associated with erotic rather than spiritual life.

COCHIN
The origin of the Christian community of Cochin goes back to the 7th century. The Cochin Christians are Nestorians. With the arrival of the Portuguese, they established ties with the Roman Church.

MADURAI
Minakshi: one of the forms of the great goddess, venerated among the Tamils of South India.

HAPPINESS IN HERAT
Herat was the center of the so-called "Timurian Renaissance" that restored Islamic civilization in Persia and India. Shah Rakh, son and successor of Timur, was governor of Herat when Clavijo, the Spanish ambassador, visited Samarkand. (On the ambience of Herat, see the memoirs of Babur.)
the wind of the hundred days: it blows in the summer.

memories of a poet-saint: the Sufi mystic and theologian Hazrat Khwaja Abdullah Ansar. A free spirit, enemy of the orthodoxy and also of superstitions. But now, in the garden which surrounds his tomb, there is an almost withered tree where devotees drive iron nails to ward off the evil eye and to cure toothaches.

the turquoise cupola: on the mausoleum of Gahar Shad, Shah Rakh's wife. It is in a park frequented every Friday by the woman of Herat.

Boddhisattva: a future Buddha, before attaining nirvana. For Hinayana Buddhism, the ideal of perfection is the Arhat, the sage who has conquered, through solitary meditation following the Buddha's example, beatitude; for the followers of Mahayana Buddhism, the ideal is the Boddhisattva who, moved by an infinite wisdom (*prajna*) and an equally infinite compassion (*karuna*), has renounced nirvana in order to help other beings on the path to illumination (*boddhi*). But the Boddhisattvas are neither gods nor saints, in the Christian and Moslem sense of the word: they are non-entities; their essence is the void (*sunyata*).

the thirty-two marks: according to the Mahayana sutras, certain signs and marks appear on the bodies of Boddhisattvas, usually 32 in number. Nevertheless, the same texts insist on the illusory nature of these marks: what distinguishes a Boddhisattva from other beings is the absence of marks.

diamond body: the essence of the Buddha is incorruptible like a diamond. Tantric Buddhism is the "path of the lightning-bolt and the diamond" (*Vajrayana*).

THE TANGHI-GARU PASS

On the old road from Kabul to Peshawar.

SHARJ TEPE

The French Archeological Mission has discovered on Sharj Tepe, a hill on the road between Pul-I-Khumari and Kunduz, a cemetery of White Huns, the nomads who, in the 4th and 5th

centuries, destroyed the Greco-Iranian-Buddhist civilization of Bactria and Gandhara and who, in the north of India, contributed to the collapse of the Gupta empire.

HIMACHAL PRADESH (1)
A state in the Western Himalayas. Some believe that the Vedic hymns were composed there.

VRINDABAN
One of the sacred cities of Hinduism, on the outskirts of Mathura, celebrated since antiquity by the followers of Krishna. According to legend, Krishna spent his childhood and youth in the forest of Vrindaban—now a barren plain—producing wonders, seducing the cowgirls, and falling in love with Radha.
saddhu: a wandering ascetic
blue tree: Krishna is blue and black, like the Mexican god Mixcoatl.
cleft stone: certain stones are symbols of the Great Goddess, particularly those whose form suggests a vulva (*yoni*).
Gone gone: the expression "Gone gone to the Other Shore" occurs frequently in the Prajnaparamita Sutra. It means: the sage has crossed over from this bank, the phenomenal world, to the other, Perfect Wisdom.

CONCERT IN THE GARDEN
Vina and mridangam: musical instruments of South India (Carnatic school).

SUNYATA
Sunyata is a term that designates the central concept of Madhyamika Buddhism: the absolute void. A radical relativism: all is relative and impermanent, not excluding the affirmation of the relativeness and impermanence of the world. The proposition that denies reality also dissolves, and thus the negation of the world by criticism is in itself a recuperation: samsara is

nirvana because all is *sunyata*. (Cf. Stcherbatsky, *Buddhist Logic*, and the commentary by Chandrakirti on Nagarjuna, *Prasanapada*, in the excellent French translation by Jacques May.)

III. TOWARD THE BEGINNING

WIND FROM ALL COMPASS POINTS
The first stanza refers to the bazaar in Kabul and the river that crosses the city; the second to a neighborhood in Paris; the others, to various places in northern India, western Pakistan, and Afghanistan.

A great flock of crows: Rubén Darío, "Song of hope #10" in *Songs of life and hope.*

Santo Domingo: the poem was written during the American intervention in the Dominican Republic.

If we had the munitions: Mexican history schoolbooks attribute this statement to General Anaya when he surrendered the Plaza de Churrubusco to General Scott, the head of the U.S. troops that invaded Mexico in 1847.

Datia: the palace-castle in the walled city of the same name, in Madhya Pradesh. Built on a black craggy promontory, it towers over the city and the plain. According to Fergusson, it is the finest example of palace architecture of the 17th century. It was built by Raja Bir Singh Deo, a military man pledged to the Emperor Jahangir. Seen from the plains, it looks like a giant iceberg of stone; half of the structure is hidden by the rock, which has been excavated to form rooms and galleries. (Cf. Percy Brown, *Indian Architecture: Islamic Period*). Datia was never inhabited, except by bats, snakes, and scorpions; its owner was assassinated before he could move in, and since then no one else has dared try. The perfect geometry of its courtyards, rooms, and galleries evokes not so much the castles of Sade, but the feverish and circular rigor of his thought. A solipsism of stone responding (corresponding) to verbal so-

lipsism. Love is inseparable from eroticism but it crosses through it unharmed.

Salang Pass: a pass in the mountains of the Hindu Kush, between Kabul and Kunduz.

Bactriana: the passage refers to this ancient province, one of the great centers of non-Mediterranean Hellenism, victim of the Kushans, the White Huns, and other invasions of nomads from Central Asia.

At the top of the world: the great god Shiva (*Mahadeva*) and Parvati, his consort, live on Mount Kailasa, in the Himalayas.

In a fig-leaf: an allusion to the children's book, *Almendrita* (Little Almond).

WITH EYES CLOSED

blind stone: a precious stone that has no transparency.

frank stone: one easy to carve.

MAITHUNA

Maithuna: the erotic couples that cover the walls of certain Buddhist and Hindu temples; sexual union; the path of illumination, in Tantric Buddhism and Hinduism, through the conjunction of *karuna* (passion) and *prajna* (wisdom). *Karuna* is the masculine side of reality and *prajna* the feminine.

Their union is *sunyata*, the void . . . empty of its emptiness.

The seventh section of the poem is an imitation of Li Po.

SUNDAY ON THE ISLAND OF ELEPHANTA

The sculpture in the 7th-century Shivaite caves of Elephanta, near Bombay, is among the most beautiful in Indian art. The reliefs represent scenes from the legends of Shiva and Parvati. The religious fervor of the Portuguese mutilated, but did not destroy, their beauty.

A TALE OF TWO GARDENS

[*Mixcoac:* Paz's childhood village, now part of Mexico City.]

[*Ajusco:* volcano in the Valley of Mexico.]

Almendrita: "Little Almond," character in the children's book of that name.

Yakshi: female deity of trees and plants.

Prajnaparamita: prajna is wisdom and *paramita* is perfection: Perfect Wisdom; the other bank; a female deity of Mahayana Buddhism, like our Sophia; woman and in Tantric Buddhism (*Vajrayana*) her vulva; the plenitude in the void.

Nagarjuna: Buddhist philosopher of the 2nd century.

Dharmakirti: Buddhist poet and logician of the 7th century.

N
I
E
G
O

NI   EGO

NIEGO = I negate/deny.
NI EGO = no(r) ego

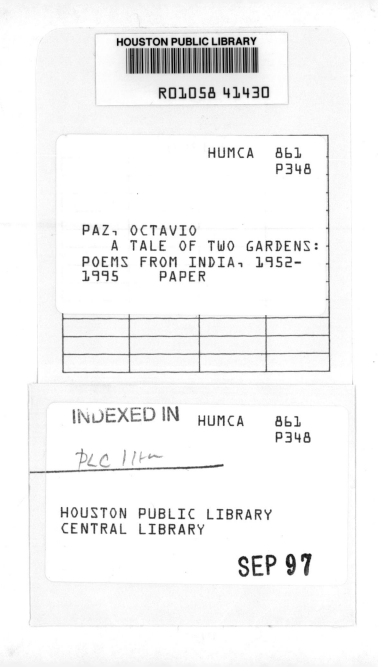